NORTHSTAR

READING AND WRITING
Basic/Low Intermediate

SECOND EDITION

Robin Mills
Laurie Frazier

Series Editors
Frances Boyd
Carol Numrich

Writing Activity Book Editor
Helen S. Solórzano

NorthStar Writing Activity Book, Basic/Low Intermediate, Second Edition

Pearson Education, 10 Bank Street, White Plains, NY 10606

Development director: Penny Laporte
Project manager: Debbie Sistino
Senior development editor: Françoise Leffler
Vice president, director of design and production: Rhea Banker
Executive managing editor: Linda Moser
Production coordinator: Melissa Leyva
Senior production editor: Kathleen Silloway
Production editor: Andréa C. Basora
Director of manufacturing: Patrice Fraccio
Senior manufacturing buyer: Dave Dickey
Cover design: Rhea Banker
Cover art: Detail of Der Rhein bei Duisburg, 1937, 145(R 5) Rhine near
    Duisburg 19 x 27.5 cm; water-based on cardboard; The Metropolitan
    Museum of Art, N.Y. The Berggruen Klee Collection, 1984.
    (1984.315.56) Photograph © 1985 The Metropolitan Museum of Art.
    © 2003 Artists Rights Society (ARS), New York / VG Bild-Kunst, Bonn
Text design: Quorum Creative Services
Text composition: Rainbow Graphics
Text font: 11/13 Sabon
Illustration credits: Duśan Petricic pp. 9, 66

Der Rhein bei Duisburg
Paul Klee

ISBN 0-321-17399-6

LONGMAN ON THE **WEB**

Longman.com offers online resources for
teachers and students. Access our Companion
Websites, our online catalog, and our local
offices around the world.

Visit us at **longman.com.**

Printed in the United States of America
4 5 6 7 8 9 10—VHG—09 08 07 06 05

Contents

Introduction

The *NorthStar Writing Activity Book,* Second Edition, is a companion to *NorthStar: Reading and Writing,* Second Edition. Building on the themes and content of the Student Book, the Writing Activity Book leads students through the writing process with engaging writing assignments. Skills and vocabulary from the Student Book are reviewed and expanded as students draft, revise, and edit their writing.

The Writing Activity Book was developed with the principle that the writing process and writing product are equally important. The units bring students step-by-step through the process of generating ideas, organizing and drafting content, revising their writing, and editing for grammar and mechanics. Students explore different prewriting techniques to find out what works best for them and for their topic. They experience the cyclical nature of writing, in which the writer is constantly evaluating and revising what is on the page. Through peer review exercises, students practice analyzing and responding to writing in a way that will help them better analyze their own writing. At the same time, they learn about the structural and rhetorical features of writing. They explore different ways to convey their ideas clearly depending on the purpose and audience of the writing assignment. They also learn how to use new grammatical structures in a meaningful context. Finally, they focus on editing and proofreading their writing for grammatical and mechanical correctness.

Design of the Units

The units are closely linked to the content of *NorthStar: Reading and Writing,* Second Edition. Therefore, it is essential that the books be used together. Each Writing Activity Book unit contains four sections that follow the writing process: Prewriting, Organizing, Revising, and Editing. The assignments are drawn from topics discussed in the Student Book readings and subsequent exercises. Teachers can choose to complete an entire unit in the Student Book before starting the writing unit. Alternatively, they can begin the Prewriting activities in the Writing Activity Book after completing the indicated sections in the Student Book and finish both units together. Checklists for the first, second, and final drafts remind students of which points to focus on in each draft.

1. Prewriting

Students complete Sections 1 to 3 in the Student Book before they begin this section. The activities in this section help students generate ideas and narrow a topic. They learn how to use a variety of prewriting techniques, such as freewriting, clustering, and brainstorming. Typically, students work together to analyze and manipulate a model prewriting exercise. Then they try using the prewriting technique on their own.

2. Organizing

In this section, students focus on organizing and developing their ideas. They learn about a structural or rhetorical feature of writing, such as writing topic and supporting sentences or organizing around a rhetorical feature, drawn from the Style section in the Student Book. They may analyze a model paragraph or organize ideas from the readings. Then they apply the ideas to their own writing. At the end of this section, students complete the first draft of the assignment and do a peer review exercise.

3. Revising

The activities in this section are designed to help students expand and polish their writing. The section has two parts. Part A, which is often drawn from the Style section in the Student Book, focuses on developing the content of students' writing. The activities help students achieve coherence and unity in their writing, clarify and improve the support for their ideas, or strengthen their introductions and conclusions. Part B, which is drawn from the Grammar section in the Student Book, helps students use the grammar point in a meaningful way in their writing. Students do exercises that use the grammar point in context. Then they look for places to apply the grammar in their writing. Although attention is given to grammatical correctness, meaningful usage is the focus. At the end of this section, students write the second draft of the assignment.

4. Editing

This section focuses on editing for grammar, form, and mechanics. Students focus on editing one feature in their writing. They identify and practice editing the feature in controlled exercises and then look for errors in their own writing. At the end of this section, students finish the final draft of the assignment.

Finding the Ideal Job

OVERVIEW	
Theme:	Work
Prewriting:	Listing
Organizing:	Understanding paragraphs and topic sentences
Revising:	Supporting the topic sentence Using adjectives to give more detail
Editing:	Formatting a paragraph

Assignment

In Unit 1 of *NorthStar: Reading and Writing,* Second Edition, you read about people who are working in their ideal jobs. What is your ideal job? The assignment for this unit is to write a paragraph describing your ideal job. You will write about why the job is ideal for you.

1 Prewriting

LISTING

 Complete Unit 1, Sections 1–3, in the Student Book before you begin this section.

It often helps to make a list of your ideas before you begin to write. When you make a list, it is not necessary to write complete sentences.

1 *Imagine you want to be a teacher. What are some reasons this may be an ideal job for you? Think about your skills, the job setting, and the job rewards. Look at the list of reasons below. Add some of your own ideas.*

Ideal Job

teacher

Reasons

like children

like to work in a school

creative

friendly co-workers

interesting work

like to help others

patient

helpful

convenient schedule

other reasons: _____

_____

_____

2 *Think about your ideal job. Why would you like that job? Think about your skills, the job setting, and job rewards. Make a list of all the reasons you can think of. It is not necessary to use complete sentences.*

2 Organizing

UNDERSTANDING PARAGRAPHS AND TOPIC SENTENCES

 Complete Unit 1, Section 4A, in the Student Book before you begin this section.

A paragraph is a group of sentences about one topic.

* The first sentence is the topic sentence. It states the main idea of the paragraph. For this assignment, the topic sentence will give the name of the writer's ideal job.

* The other sentences are supporting sentences. They explain the main idea with specific details and examples. For this assignment, the supporting sentences will give reasons why the writer likes his or her ideal job.

1 *Read the example paragraph and complete the tasks below.*

I would like to be a mountain climbing guide. I like this job for several reasons. First of all, mountain climbing is very exciting. Mountain climbing guides get to climb tall, dangerous mountains. Second, I enjoy working outside. I like the fresh air much better than I like a stuffy office. Finally, I like to meet interesting people. Mountain climbing guides travel to many different parts of the world and meet other adventurous people.

1. Circle the topic sentence. What is the writer's ideal job?

2. Underline the supporting sentences. What three reasons does the writer give for liking the job?

2 *Read the paragraph and choose the best topic sentence from the list below. Write the sentence on the line. Remember that the topic sentence must give the name of the writer's ideal job.*

_____.
There are many reasons why I like this job. First, I like animals. Animals bring a lot of joy to our lives, but they do not ask for a lot in return. I also enjoy helping animals and their owners feel better. Pet owners are happy when their pets are well. Finally, veterinarians get to work with other people who like animals. They can even bring their pets to work!

Topic Sentences

Sometimes I imagine I'm a veterinarian.
I would like a job working with animals.
A veterinarian helps people and animals feel better.

WRITING THE FIRST DRAFT

Use the information from the previous sections to write the first draft of your paragraph.

• Begin your paragraph with a topic sentence, such as "Sometimes I imagine that I am a(n) . . ." or "I would like to be a(n) . . ."

• Look at the list you wrote for Exercise 2 on page 2. Choose the three most important reasons you listed. Write a complete sentence for each reason.

Don't worry too much about grammar. Just try to make your ideas clear.

PEER REVIEW

When you finish your first draft, exchange papers with another student. Read your partner's first draft and answer the questions below. Then discuss your answers with your partner.

• Does the paragraph begin with a topic sentence?

• Does the paragraph include at least three reasons why the writer likes his or her ideal job?

• Are there any words or sentences that you don't understand? Circle those parts that the writer should explain more clearly.

Discuss your partner's reaction to your paragraph. Make a note of any parts you need to revise.

---

3 Revising

A SUPPORTING THE TOPIC SENTENCE

The supporting sentences in your paragraph should all relate to the main idea. They should all support the topic sentence.

1 *Read the paragraph. Cross out sentences that don't support the main idea.*

> Sometimes I imagine that I am a teacher. I like this job for several reasons. First, I love children. I like to help children learn and grow. Sometimes children are difficult to work with because they don't always listen and follow directions. Second, teaching is a creative job. Artists are creative too, so I would also like to be an artist. Finally, the schedule is convenient for me. But I don't like the salary, because teachers don't make very much money.

2 *Look at your first draft. Cross out sentences that don't support the main idea. If necessary, write new sentences that support the main idea.*

B USING ADJECTIVES TO GIVE MORE DETAIL

 Complete Unit 1, Section 4B, in the Student Book before you begin this section.

Descriptive adjectives give detail to your writing. They make your ideas clear to the reader.

1 *Read the sentences. Underline the descriptive adjectives.*

1. Good teachers are creative.

2. They teach interesting classes.

3. They are also patient and caring.

2 *Write two or three sentences about people in the following professions. Use the descriptive adjectives below or think of other adjectives. When you have finished, share your sentences with the class.*

Professions

artists   corporate CEOs

computer programmers   athletes

Descriptive Adjectives

busy	rich	intelligent
young	famous	well-educated
strong	motivated	interesting
powerful	patient	
successful	creative	
hardworking	independent	

3 *Look at your first draft. Did you use any descriptive adjectives? Add adjectives if they will help make your meaning clear.*

WRITING THE SECOND DRAFT

Now you are ready to write your second draft. Look at all your notes from the previous sections to help you revise.

- Include sentences that support the main idea.

- Add detail with descriptive adjectives to make your ideas clear to the reader.

4 Editing

FORMATTING A PARAGRAPH

Look at the paragraph below. Read the rules for formatting a paragraph.

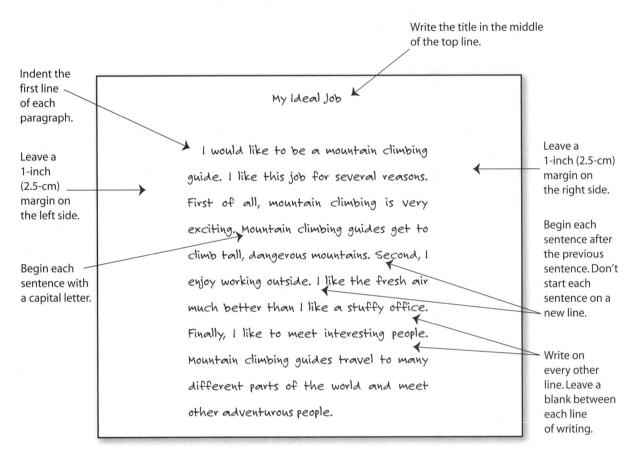

Write the title in the middle of the top line.

Indent the first line of each paragraph.

Leave a 1-inch (2.5-cm) margin on the left side.

Begin each sentence with a capital letter.

Leave a 1-inch (2.5-cm) margin on the right side.

Begin each sentence after the previous sentence. Don't start each sentence on a new line.

Write on every other line. Leave a blank between each line of writing.

My Ideal Job

I would like to be a mountain climbing guide. I like this job for several reasons. First of all, mountain climbing is very exciting. Mountain climbing guides get to climb tall, dangerous mountains. Second, I enjoy working outside. I like the fresh air much better than I like a stuffy office. Finally, I like to meet interesting people. Mountain climbing guides travel to many different parts of the world and meet other adventurous people.

1 *Read the paragraph below. There are mistakes in paragraph format. Rewrite the paragraph on a separate sheet of paper. Discuss your corrections with the class.*

> **My Ideal Job**
>
> Sometimes I imagine that I am a teacher. I like this job for several reasons.
>
> First, I love children. I like to help children learn and grow. Children are fun to work with because they like to laugh and play games.
>
> Second, teaching is a creative job. Teachers think of new and interesting ways to learn.
>
> Finally, the schedule is convenient for me. teachers can take long vacations in the summer.

2 *Look at your second draft. Is it formatted correctly? Mark any mistakes in paragraph format. Add a title to your paragraph.*

PREPARING THE FINAL DRAFT

Carefully edit your second draft. Use the checklist below as a guide. Then neatly write or type your paragraph with the corrections.

FINAL DRAFT CHECKLIST

- ❏ Does the topic sentence state the main idea of the paragraph?
- ❏ Do you give at least three reasons why you like your ideal job?
- ❏ Do all the sentences support the main idea?
- ❏ Do you use descriptive adjectives to add detail?
- ❏ Is the paragraph formatted correctly?

UNIT 2

Country Life vs. City Life

OVERVIEW

Theme:	The country and the city
Prewriting:	Using pictures
Organizing:	Grouping details
Revising:	Adding supporting details
	Writing about past events
Editing:	Using commas and periods

Assignment

In Unit 2 of *NorthStar: Reading and Writing,* Second Edition, you read about farm life versus city life. Have you ever been to a farm or another area in the country? Did you enjoy it? Or do you prefer the city? The assignment for this unit is to write a paragraph describing a farm, nature area, or city you have visited. You will write about what this farm, nature area, or city looked like; what you did there; and how you felt about the place.

1 Prewriting

USING PICTURES

 Complete Unit 2, Sections 1–3, in the Student Book before you begin this section.

Drawing a picture of a place can help you remember details.

1 *Look at the picture. What kind of nature area is this? Is it in the country, in a city, in the suburbs, or on a farm? What do you see in the picture?*

2 *Work with a partner. Write the adjectives beside the things they describe. Then add some adjectives of your own.*

Adjectives

active   happy   large   green

tall   relaxed   popular   modern

Things in the Picture

lake *popular* _____   people _____

park _____   trees _____

buildings _____   animals _____

3 *Think of a farm, nature area, or city that you have visited. The nature area can be a large place, such as a wildlife park or mountain, or it can be a small place, such as a city park or backyard garden. On a separate piece of paper, draw a picture of the place. Don't worry about how good your drawing is. Just try to draw as many details as you can.*

4 *Look at your picture and, on a separate piece of paper, make a list of the things you see. Then write adjectives to describe them.*

2 Organizing

GROUPING DETAILS

When you describe a place, you should group similar details together. You can arrange the information in your paragraph into four parts:

- Where you went
- What you did there
- What you saw
- How you felt

1 *Imagine you recently visited the park shown on page 9. Call it West Park. Use the words and phrases below to describe your visit. Write each word or phrase in the correct place in the chart.*

the lake	people walking and jogging
happy	ducks and geese
people riding bikes	looked around
buildings	people fishing
boats	relaxed
walked	people in-line skating
jogged	squirrels
people boating	rode my bike

Where you went	West Park
What you did there	
What you saw	
How you felt	

2 *Now look at your own picture and the lists you made in Exercise 4 on page 9. Draw a chart like the one above on a separate piece of paper. Fill in the chart with the information about your place.*

WRITING THE FIRST DRAFT

Use the information from the previous sections to write the first draft of your paragraph.

- Start your paragraph with a topic sentence. Include the name and location of the place you are describing. Begin the sentence: "Last (week, month, year) I went to . . ."

- Group similar details together: what you did, what you saw, how you felt.

- Use adjectives for description.

- End your paragraph with a sentence like: "For all these reasons, I enjoyed going to . . ."

Don't worry too much about grammar. Just try to make your ideas clear.

PEER REVIEW

When you finish your first draft, exchange papers with another student. Read your partner's first draft and answer the questions below. Then discuss your answers with your partner.

- Does the paragraph give the name and location of the place your partner visited?

- Does the paragraph tell what the writer did, saw, and felt?

- Does the writer use adjectives to describe the place? Underline anything the writer can describe with adjectives.

Discuss your partner's reaction to your paragraph. Make a note of any parts you need to revise.

---

3 Revising

A ADDING SUPPORTING DETAILS

 Complete Unit 2, Section 4A, in the Student Book before you begin this section.

Details help the reader see a clear picture of the place you are describing. You can add supporting details by telling exactly where people and things are located, what they are doing, and what they look like.

1 *Look at the topic sentences below. Check (✓) the three details that best support the main idea.*

a. Yesterday I went to a beautiful lake in our town.

_____ Sometimes I rent a boat at the boathouse there.

_____ There are lots of ducks living on the lake.

_____ There are trails around the lake for walking and jogging.

_____ I don't have a lot of time to visit the lake.

b. I enjoyed going to my parents' home in the mountains.

_____ I always felt very relaxed there.

_____ I enjoyed shopping at the mall.

_____ The mountains were so quiet, and life seemed so slow.

_____ The fresh air made me feel healthy.

c. The city park is a wonderful place to visit.

_____ You can see many beautiful flowers and trees.

_____ The birds are always a pleasure to watch.

_____ The park was built in 1962.

_____ It's fun to watch people walking, jogging, or riding their bicycles.

2 *Look at your first draft. Underline some places where you could add more supporting details. Write some new sentences to add to your paragraph.*

B   WRITING ABOUT PAST EVENTS

Complete Unit 2, Section 4B, in the Student Book before you begin this section.

In your paragraph, you are describing what you did and saw in the past. To describe an event in the past, you need to use the simple past tense.

1 *Complete the paragraph, using the simple past form of the verbs.*

Last summer, I visited my cousin's farm in Montana. I _____

1. (stay)

with my cousin's family in their house. It's a beautiful old farmhouse. During

the day, we _____ my uncle work on the farm. We
                  2. (help)
_____ the animals and _____ the vegetables. In
      3. (feed)   **4.** (water)
the afternoons, we _____ the horses out for a ride. We
                          5. (take)
_____ through the mountains near their farm. From the top of
      6. (ride)
the mountain, we _____ the farm. I live in the city, so visiting
                        7. (see)
the farm _____ different for me. It was a lot of hard work, but
              8. (be)
it was fun too. I _____ very tired at the end of every day, but I
                        9. (feel)
was happy to work so hard. I love farm work. I think I could really get used

to life on a farm.

2 *Look at your first draft. Did you use the simple past tense to describe events that happened in the past? Underline the verbs and make sure you used the correct form.*

WRITING THE SECOND DRAFT

Now you are ready to write your second draft. Look at all your notes from the previous sections to help you revise.

* Add supporting details about the place you visited.

* Use the simple past tense to describe past events.

4 Editing

USING COMMAS AND PERIODS

* Use commas to separate items in a list.

  I like to go hiking, swimming, and bird-watching.

* Use a period at the end of a sentence.

  There are many reasons why I enjoy going to the mountains.

1 *Read the paragraph. Write the correct punctuation in each space. Use commas and periods.*

Last Saturday, I went to a park in my neighborhood_____ It was a beautiful day_____ The park was very crowded. It was full of children_____ adults_____ and dogs_____ My friend and I rode our bikes to the park_____ played some Frisbee_____ and had a picnic lunch_____ Then we went home_____ It was a fun afternoon.

2 *Look at your second draft and edit the punctuation. Do you use commas and periods in the correct places?*

PREPARING THE FINAL DRAFT

Carefully edit your second draft. Use the checklist below as a guide. Then neatly write or type your paragraph with the corrections.

FINAL DRAFT CHECKLIST

- ❏ Do you include the name and location of the area you visited?
- ❏ Do you group the details according to where you went, what you did there, what you saw, and how you felt?
- ❏ Do you use adjectives and supporting details?
- ❏ Do you use the simple past tense to describe past events?
- ❏ Do you use commas and periods correctly?

Making Money

OVERVIEW

Theme:	Money
Prewriting:	Making a chart
Organizing:	Comparing and contrasting
Revising:	Giving explanations
	Making comparisons with adjectives
Editing:	Punctuating transition words of addition and contrast

Assignment

In Unit 3 of *NorthStar: Reading and Writing,* Second Edition, you read about counterfeit money. What other products can be illegally counterfeited? How can you tell the difference between a real and a counterfeit product? The assignment for this unit is to write a paragraph comparing a real product to a counterfeit product. You will explain how the two products are different.

1 Prewriting

MAKING A CHART

Complete Unit 3, Sections 1–3, in the Student Book before you begin this section.

A chart can help you see the differences between a counterfeit product and a real product.

1 *Look at the chart below. It contrasts counterfeit money and real money. Complete the chart with the following information from the readings in the Student Book.*

color-changing ink

regular computer paper

legal

Product: Money

DIFFERENCES	COUNTERFEIT MONEY	REAL MONEY
1. Paper		special paper
2. Ink	regular ink	
3. Printing process	no microprint	microprint
4. Laws	illegal	
5. Security	XXXXX	equipment to check for counterfeit money

2 *With the class, think of other products that people counterfeit. Make a list of products on the board. Possible products include designer clothing, watches, audio- or videotapes, music CDs, software, and computers.*

3 *Choose one product that you want to write about. Make a list of things that you can compare, such as material, design, and color.*

4 *Contrast the counterfeit product to the real product. Think about the differences between the counterfeit product and the real product. Fill in the chart below with as many differences as you can. Add more rows if you need them.*

Product: _____

DIFFERENCES	COUNTERFEIT _____	REAL _____
1.		
2.		
3.		
4.		
5.		

2 Organizing

COMPARING AND CONTRASTING

 Complete Unit 3, Section 4A, in the Student Book before you begin this section.

A comparison and contrast paragraph describes how two things are similar or different. This assignment focuses on the differences between a real product and a counterfeit product. It is important to organize your paragraph so that the differences are clear to the reader.

- Describe each difference one by one.

- Use the transition words *however* and *in contrast* to introduce an opposite idea.

- Use the transition words *in addition, also,* and *too* to add a similar idea.

1 *Read the paragraph and complete the tasks below.*

> There are several important differences between real money and counterfeit money. First, the paper is different. Real money uses special paper. In contrast, counterfeit money uses regular computer paper. In addition, the ink is different. Real money uses color-changing ink. However, counterfeit money uses regular ink. The printing methods are also different. Real money has microprint. In contrast, counterfeit money doesn't have microprint. By looking for these features, you can see the differences between real money and counterfeit money.

1. What is the topic sentence of the paragraph? Underline it.

2. What three differences are explained in the paragraph? Circle them.

3. Check the transition words of addition and contrast. What idea does each transition word introduce?

2 *Look at the ideas in your chart on page 17. Which differences are the most important or interesting? Choose three differences to write about in your paragraph. Write the information about the differences on a separate piece of paper.*

Example

Product: _Money_

Difference: _Paper_

Real product: _Special paper_

Counterfeit product: _Regular computer paper_

WRITING THE FIRST DRAFT

Use the information from the previous sections to write the first draft of your paragraph.

• Write a topic sentence that names the product you are writing about.

- Describe three differences between the real and counterfeit products.
- Use transition words of addition and contrast.

Don't worry too much about grammar. Just try to make your ideas clear.

PEER REVIEW

When you finish your first draft, exchange papers with another student. Read your partner's first draft and answer the questions below. Then discuss your answers with your partner.

- What does the writer compare?

- What differences does the writer mention?

- Can you think of more features the writer can write about?

- Does the writer use transition words of addition and contrast? Circle the transition words.

Discuss your partner's reaction to your paragraph. Make a note of any parts you need to revise.

---

3 Revising

A GIVING EXPLANATIONS

You need to clearly explain the differences between the real and counterfeit product. To do so, you must explain any important ideas or words you used to describe the differences. A reader might ask these questions about the paragraph on counterfeit money on page 18.

- What is microprint?
- What is color-changing ink?
- Why is the paper special?

1 *Add more explanation to the paragraph using information from the readings. Decide where the following explanations should go in the paragraph. Then write them in the spaces.*

Explanations

looks yellow from one angle and green from another

is the use of small words hidden in the design

has red and blue silk in it

There are several important differences between real money and counterfeit money. First, the paper is different. Real money uses special paper. The special paper _____. In contrast, counterfeit money uses regular computer paper. In addition, the ink is different. Real money uses color-changing ink. Color-changing ink _____. However, counterfeit money uses regular ink. The printing methods are also different. Real money has microprint. Microprint _____ _____. In contrast, counterfeit money doesn't have microprint. By looking for these features, you can see the differences between real money and counterfeit money.

---

2 *Work in pairs. With your partner, look at the first draft of your paragraph. Find any important ideas or words that you need to explain to your reader and list them on a separate piece of paper. Then write an explanation for each one and add the explanations to your paragraph.*

B MAKING COMPARISONS WITH ADJECTIVES

Complete Unit 3, Section 4B, in the Student Book before you begin this section.

You can use comparative adjectives to talk about the differences between a real product and a counterfeit product.

1 *Complete the sentences with comparative adjectives. Choose the most appropriate adjective in parentheses.*

1. Real money is made on special paper. The paper has red and blue silk in it. The silk makes the paper rough. However, counterfeit money uses regular paper without silk. The paper is smooth. The paper for real money is

   _____ than the paper for counterfeit money.
   (rough/smooth)

2. Store owners can buy equipment to test counterfeit money. Stores have currency validator pens and electronic cash scanners to find counterfeit money. This makes it difficult to spend counterfeit money. It is _____
   (difficult/easy)
   to spend real money than counterfeit money.

2 *Look at your first draft. Did you use any comparative adjectives? If you did, are they used correctly? If you did not, find one or two places where you can add a comparison using comparative adjectives.*

WRITING THE SECOND DRAFT

Now you are ready to write your second draft. Look at all your notes from the previous sections to help you revise.

* Explain any important ideas or words that the reader needs to understand.

* Use comparative adjectives to make comparisons.

4 Editing

PUNCTUATING TRANSITION WORDS OF ADDITION AND CONTRAST

Transition words of addition and contrast can be used to connect sentences when you compare two things.

1 *The four transition words of addition and contrast in this paragraph need punctuation. First, underline the transition words. Then add a comma if necessary.*

There are several important differences between real money and counterfeit money. First, the paper is different. Real money uses special paper. The special paper has red and blue silk in it. In addition it has a line that you can see with an ultraviolet light. In contrast counterfeit money uses regular computer paper. The regular paper is smoother than the paper with silk in it. Second, the ink is different. Real money uses color-changing ink. Color-changing ink looks yellow from one angle and green from another. However counterfeit money uses regular ink. Finally, the printing methods are different. Real money has microprint. Microprint is the use of small words hidden in the design. It is more difficult to copy money with microprint than money without microprint. In contrast counterfeit money doesn't have microprint. By looking for these features, you can see the differences between real money and counterfeit money.

2 *Look at your second draft. Is the punctuation with transition words of addition and contrast correct? Make corrections.*

PREPARING THE FINAL DRAFT

Carefully edit your second draft. Use the checklist below as a guide. Then neatly write or type your paragraph with the corrections.

FINAL DRAFT CHECKLIST

- ❏ Do you describe three differences between the counterfeit product and the real product?
- ❏ Do you explain any important words that the reader needs to know?
- ❏ Do you use transition words of addition and contrast?
- ❏ Are the comparative adjectives used correctly?
- ❏ Is the punctuation for transition words correct?

Save the Elephants

OVERVIEW

Theme:	Animals
Prewriting:	Brainstorming
Organizing:	Persuading the reader
Revising:	Explaining reasons
	Asking *Wh-* questions
Editing:	Formatting a letter

Assignment

In Unit 4 of *NorthStar: Reading and Writing,* Second Edition, you read about saving endangered animals. What are some endangered animals you know about? Do you think it is important to save them? Why or why not? The assignment for this unit is to write a letter to the editor of a local newspaper. You will explain why you think we should or should not try to save one of the endangered animals, and you will try to persuade (convince) the reader to agree with your opinion.

1 Prewriting

BRAINSTORMING

 Complete Unit 4, Sections 1–3, in the Student Book before you begin this section.

Brainstorming can help you get ideas for your writing. In brainstorming, you think of as many ideas as possible about a topic. No ideas are bad or wrong. You can brainstorm alone or with other people.

1 *With your teacher and the rest of the class, brainstorm the names of animals that are endangered. Write these names on the board.*

2 *Look at the brainstorming ideas about endangered elephants. Add your own ideas. Write down any words or phrases that come to your mind about endangered elephants.*

Endangered elephants

hunters   ivory   tusks   eucalyptus trees

3 *On your own, choose one endangered animal you want to write about. It can be an animal you think should be saved or an animal you don't think needs to be saved. Write the name of the endangered animal in the middle of a piece of paper. Brainstorm about this animal. Write down any words or phrases you think of.*

2 Organizing

PERSUADING THE READER

Complete Unit 4, Section 4A, in the Student Book before you begin this section.

The purpose of your letter is to *persuade* (or convince) the reader to agree with your opinion. You can do three things to persuade your reader:

* Explain who you are and why you are writing the letter (give your opinion). Look at the beginning of the letter "Save a Logger—Eat an Owl" in Unit 4, Section 2B, of the Student Book.

  I am really angry about the article on the spotted owl. The article talked only about saving the owl. But what about us—the loggers?

  The beginning tells us who is writing the letter and why he is writing it. The writer starts to persuade us because he knows something about the problem and he states his opinion clearly.

* Give persuasive reasons to support your opinion.

* Explain your reasons with details and examples.

1 *Read the first parts of letters about saving the tiger, and answer the questions below.*

  1. I am a student at the University of California. I am majoring in ecology studies. I am writing because we need to save the wild tigers.

  2. Many people care about endangered animals. People argue about how to save them. It's a complicated problem.

3. I am a student from northern India. Wild tigers live in the forest near my home. I believe we should stop cutting the forest and save the wild tigers.

4. I have read about saving the wild tigers. I love nature and care about all animals. We should not let the tigers become extinct.

5. I'm a student. I think that we should save the wild tigers.

- Does the writer tell who he or she is?

- Does the writer explain why he or she is writing the letter?

- Which letters do you think will be most persuasive? Why?

2 *Write two or three sentences explaining who you are and why you are writing your letter. Clearly state your opinion about the endangered animal.*

3 *A persuasive reason convinces people to agree with you. Work with a partner. Read the opinions below and the reasons to support the opinions. For each opinion, put a check (✓) next to the three reasons that are the most persuasive. Then discuss the questions.*

Opinion 1: We must save the endangered wild tigers.

_____ Hunters kill tigers and sell their fur.

_____ Tigers are beautiful animals.

_____ Tigers are an important part of our ecology.

_____ There are several kinds of tigers.

_____ Today there are only between 5,000 and 7,000 wild tigers in the world.

Opinion 2: Saving the wild tigers is hurting people.

_____ Tigers are large, striped cats.

_____ Tigers hunt and kill people.

_____ Many people make money from selling tiger skins and other parts.

_____ I am afraid of tigers.

_____ People cannot have farms where tigers live.

- What is persuasive about some of the reasons?

- What is not persuasive about others?

- In which order would you put the persuasive reasons in a paragraph? Number the persuasive reasons from 1 to 3.

4 *Look back at your brainstorming in Exercise 3 on page 24. Think of two or three persuasive reasons to save or not save the endangered animal.*

WRITING THE FIRST DRAFT

Use the information from the previous sections to write the first draft of your letter.

- Write two or three introductory sentences. Explain who you are and why you are writing the letter. State your opinion clearly.

- Write a paragraph giving two or three persuasive reasons the reader should agree with you.

- Explain your reasons with details and examples. (You will work more on your explanation in the next section.)

Don't worry too much about grammar. Just try to make your ideas clear.

PEER REVIEW

When you finish your first draft, exchange letters with another student. Read your partner's first draft and answer the questions below. Then discuss your answers with your partner.

- Does the letter have introductory sentences? Do they give the writer's opinion about saving an animal? Does the writer tell something about himself or herself?

- How many reasons are there to support the writer's opinion?

- Are the reasons explained persuasively? Underline any parts of the explanations that could be more persuasive.

Discuss your partner's reaction to your letter. Make a note of any parts you need to revise.

---

3 Revising

A EXPLAINING REASONS

You can make your point stronger by using specific details and examples. Make sure the details and examples support your opinion.

1 *Read the opinions and supporting reasons below. Which explanations are most persuasive? Do the details and examples support the opinion? Put a check (✓) next to the explanation that is most persuasive for each reason. Discuss why it is more persuasive than the other explanations.*

1. Wild tigers are in danger. We don't have much time to save them.

_____ There aren't very many tigers. Soon all the tigers will be gone. That will be very sad.

_____ Other animals are endangered too. There are only 3,600 northern spotted owls and 1,000 pandas.

_____ Today there are only between 5,000 and 7,000 wild tigers in the world. One hundred years ago there were over 100,000 tigers. Some experts say that in ten years, wild tigers will be extinct.

2. White dolphins are endangered and we must save them. Dolphins are very intelligent animals.

_____ Dolphins can learn tricks to entertain people. They can jump up in the air, catch things in their mouths, and dance in the water. They are fun to watch.

_____ Dolphins can communicate with each other. Some people believe that we will be able to talk to them some day. We should study and protect the animals so that we can learn more about them.

_____ Many other animals are intelligent as well. For example, some chimpanzees learned how to speak sign language.

2 *Look at your first draft. Find places where you can make your reasons more convincing by adding details and examples. Use the comments from the peer review and your teacher to help you. Add the new information to your draft.*

B ASKING *Wh-* QUESTIONS

Complete Unit 4, Section 4B, in the Student Book before you begin this section.

Questions can be used to emphasize important information. The question makes the reader pay more attention to what you are saying. Look at the example questions and answers below. They are taken from the readings.

• The paper companies make a lot of money from the eucalyptus trees. *But what about the elephants? They can't eat eucalyptus trees!*

• But by 1992, we were cutting only 100,000 feet of wood per year. *Why? Because people like you who just care about the owls stopped us from doing our jobs.*

1 *Use the words to write questions. The first one has been done for you.*

tigers/how many/there/are   *How many tigers are there?* _____

we/save them/why/should _____

they/how/are/important _____

what/you/do/can _____

2 *The following paragraph is the body of a letter. Add three of the questions you wrote in Exercise 1 to the paragraph to get the reader's attention.*

> We must act now to save the endangered wild tigers. _____
> _____ First, tigers are beautiful animals.
> They are the biggest cats in the world. They are known everywhere for their
> beautiful orange and black striped fur. In addition, tigers are an important
> part of our ecology. _____ They hunt and kill
> small animals such as rats and rabbits. Without tigers, the number of small
> animals would increase and cause problems for people. Finally, we don't
> have much time to save the tigers. _____
> There are only between 5,000 and 7,000 wild tigers in the world today. One
> hundred years ago there were over 100,000 tigers. Some experts say that in
> ten years, wild tigers will be extinct. _____
> Join the fight to save the endangered wild tigers!

3 *Look at your first draft. Find one place in your letter where you can add a question to get the reader's attention. Write a question and add it to the letter.*

WRITING THE SECOND DRAFT

Now you are ready to write your second draft. Look at all your notes from the previous sections to help you revise.

- Give details and examples to support your reasons for saving or not saving the endangered animal.

- Write *Wh-* questions and answers to introduce important sections of the letter.

- Use any feedback from your partner to give more information about the problems.

4 Editing

FORMATTING A LETTER

You are writing a letter to the editor of a local newspaper. The letter should be formatted like a business letter. It should have six parts:

Date

Name and address of the writer

Opening

Body

Closing

Signature

1 *Look at the second draft of your letter. Did you include all the parts? Is it formatted correctly? Correct any formatting mistakes.*

2 *There are different openings and closings for different types of letters. Circle the openings and closings that could be used in a letter to the editor. Discuss why the others cannot be used. Then add an opening and closing to your draft.*

Openings	**Closings**
Dear Joe,	Love,
Dear Editor:	Sincerely,
To Whom It May Concern:	Yours truly,

PREPARING THE FINAL DRAFT

Carefully edit your second draft. Use the checklist below as a guide. Then neatly write or type your paragraph with the corrections.

FINAL DRAFT CHECKLIST

❑ Do you explain who you are and why you care about the problem?

❑ Do you give two or three persuasive reasons to save the endangered animal?

❑ Do you explain your reasons with details and examples?

❑ Do you use a question to catch the reader's attention?

❑ Is the letter formatted correctly?

UNIT 5

"Netiquette"

OVERVIEW	
Theme:	Network etiquette
Prewriting:	Making a tree diagram
Organizing:	Giving examples
Revising:	Developing paragraph unity
	Using verbs plus gerunds and infinitives
Editing:	Using commas or colons

Assignment

In Unit 5 of *NorthStar: Reading and Writing,* Second Edition, you read about netiquette (network etiquette or e-mail etiquette). What are the advantages and disadvantages of communicating with technology such as e-mail? The assignment for this unit is to write a paragraph about one technology used for communication, such as e-mail, the Internet, pagers, cell phones, or instant messaging. You will explain the advantages and disadvantages of the technology.

1 Prewriting

MAKING A TREE DIAGRAM

 Complete Unit 5, Sections 1–3, in the Student Book before you begin this section.

A tree diagram helps connect ideas to a main topic the way branches of a tree connect to its trunk.

1 *Look at the following tree diagram about the advantages and disadvantages of e-mail. E-mail represents the trunk or the main topic. One branch shows the advantages and the other branch shows the disadvantages.*

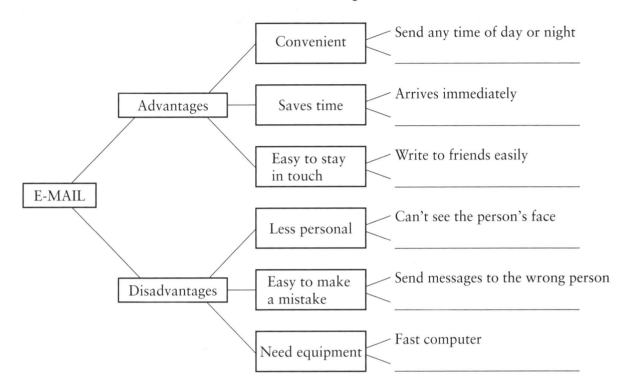

2 *Here are some more advantages and disadvantages of e-mail. Add the information to the tree diagram.*

- Can't hear a person's tone of voice
- Cheaper than a phone call
- Computer modem to connect to the Internet
- Fast answers to messages
- Send private information by mistake
- Write to several people at the same time

3 *Choose one technology to write about (e-mail, Internet, pagers, cell phones, instant messaging, etc). Make a tree diagram like the example above. Show the advantages and disadvantages of the technology. Give examples to illustrate each advantage and disadvantage.*

2 Organizing

GIVING EXAMPLES

To illustrate the advantages and disadvantages of e-mail, you need to give examples. Your examples will be effective if they are placed directly after the statements they illustrate and if they include specific details.

1 *Work with a partner. Read the statements below. Check (✓) the specific details that go with the statements.*

1. E-mail is very convenient. You can send it any time of day or night.

_____ You can work when everyone is sleeping.

_____ You don't need stamps.

_____ You can work when you have time.

2. You need special equipment.

_____ You need a computer.

_____ You can't hear the person's voice.

_____ You need to have an Internet service provider.

2 *Complete the paragraph on page 33 with appropriate sentences that give examples. Choose from the sentences in the box.*

I often get an immediate reply.

You can't hear a person's tone of voice in e-mail.

You can choose the wrong e-mail address if you are not careful and send the e-mail to the wrong person.

I know people who live in many parts of the world, and I can send e-mail to all of them.

There are advantages and disadvantages to using e-mail. One advantage is that e-mail is very fast. _____

_____

It is also a good way to stay in touch with family and friends. _____

_____

One disadvantage of e-mail is that it is easy to make mistakes. _____

_____

In addition, e-mail is less personal than a phone call. _____

_____

3 *Look back at your tree diagram (page 31). Choose two advantages and two disadvantages that you want to write about. Then choose two or three examples for each. Think of specific details to help illustrate your examples.*

WRITING THE FIRST DRAFT

Use the information from the previous sections to write the first draft of your paragraph.

* Write a topic sentence like this:

  There are advantages and disadvantages to two-way pagers.

  Cell phones have advantages and disadvantages.

* List two advantages and two disadvantages.
* Give examples of the advantages and disadvantages. Introduce your examples with *For example* or *For instance.*
* Include specific details in your examples.

Don't worry too much about grammar. Just try to make your ideas clear.

PEER REVIEW

When you finish your first draft, exchange papers with another student. Read your partner's first draft and answer the questions below. Then discuss your answers with your partner.

- What are the advantages and disadvantages of the technology your partner chose?

- Are there examples to illustrate each advantage and disadvantage?

- Do the examples include specific details? Underline three details that best illustrate the advantages and disadvantages.

Discuss your partner's reaction to your paragraph. Make a note of any parts you need to revise.

---

3 Revising

A DEVELOPING PARAGRAPH UNITY

A paragraph has unity when all the supporting sentences are connected to the topic sentence. None of the supporting sentences are about other topics.

1 *Each paragraph should mention advantages and disadvantages of one technology. Read the topic sentence. Look at the list of advantages and disadvantages. Cross out the two sentences that do not support the topic sentence.*

Topic sentence:	E-mail has advantages and disadvantages.
Advantages:	a. You can send an e-mail message at any time.
	b. Computers are very useful.
	c. E-mail is very fast.
Disadvantages:	d. Long-distance telephone calls are expensive.
	e. You can send an e-mail message to the wrong person by mistake.
	f. You need a computer to use e-mail.

2 *Read the following paragraph and complete the tasks below.*

Two-way text pagers have advantages and disadvantages. One advantage is that they are convenient. Many of my friends have them, so we can stay in touch all day long. However, my mother doesn't have one, so I have to call her on the telephone. Another advantage is that they are quiet. My friend has a pager that makes a lot of funny noises. You can send and receive messages anywhere without making a sound. One disadvantage of two-way text pagers is that the keys are very small. It's hard to type the correct letters, so sometimes I type the wrong words. I wish I took typing in college. In addition, the print is small. It is difficult to read the messages, especially in a dark room. It's easier to read messages on the computer. Sometimes my eyes hurt when I read a lot of text messages on my pager.

1. Circle the topic sentence.

2. Underline the sentences stating the two advantages and two disadvantages.

3. Read the examples that illustrate each advantage and disadvantage. Cross out the four sentences that do not illustrate the advantages and disadvantages.

3 *Look at the first draft of your paragraph. Are there any sentences that do not support the main idea stated in the topic sentence? If so, cross them out. Add more supporting sentences if necessary.*

B   USING VERBS PLUS GERUNDS AND INFINITIVES

Complete Unit 5, Section 4B, in the Student Book before you begin this section.

Some verbs are followed by a gerund and some are followed by an infinitive.

Examples

I *like* **to use** e-mail.

I *enjoy* **getting** a lot of e-mail every day.

1 *Complete the sentences below with phrases from the box. Use an infinitive or gerund as appropriate. There is more than one correct answer.*

> get lots of e-mail from friends
>
> learn e-mail emoticons
>
> learn to use e-mail
>
> receive spam e-mail
>
> send letters, so e-mail is easier
>
> stay in touch with friends
>
> talk to their family on the phone
>
> write letters when they start using e-mail

1. Some people don't like _____.

2. Many people want _____.

3. I enjoy _____.

4. Many people stop _____.

5. I often forget _____.

6. You can try _____.

7. My friend recommends _____.

8. I prefer _____.

2 *Look at the first draft of your paragraph. Underline the verbs that are followed by a gerund or infinitive. Did you use the correct verb form following those words?*

WRITING THE SECOND DRAFT

Now you are ready to write your second draft. Look at all your notes from the previous sections to help you revise.

- Make sure you have paragraph unity. Make sure all your examples illustrate the advantages and disadvantages mentioned in your paragraph.

- Use gerunds or infinitives as appropriate.

4 Editing

USING COMMAS OR COLONS

 Complete Unit 5, Section 4A, in the Student Book before you begin this section.

1 *Look at the use of commas and colons.*

Use commas:

* to separate parts of a sentence

  I have a cell phone, but I don't have a two-way text pager.

* to separate three or more items in a list

  Sending e-mail is convenient, fast, and inexpensive.

* with numbers larger than 999

  A good computer costs more than $1,000.

Use a colon:

* to introduce a list

  There are many things to do on the Internet: send e-mail, find information on the Web, or download music.

2 *Put a comma or colon where necessary in these sentences.*

1. E-mail has several disadvantages it takes too much time it is not personal and there are too many misunderstandings.

2. My sister mother and brother all use cell phones.

3. Pagers are fast easy and fun to use.

4. I like to stay up late listen to music and answer all my e-mail.

5. There are some disadvantages to e-mail I can't type I don't have an e-mail address and I don't have a computer.

6. My family lives more than 3000 miles away. I can still stay in touch by e-mail.

3 *Look at your second draft. Where necessary, add commas or colons.*

PREPARING THE FINAL DRAFT

Carefully edit your second draft. Use the checklist below as a guide. Then neatly write or type your paragraph with the corrections.

FINAL DRAFT CHECKLIST

❏ Do you describe the advantages and disadvantages of a technology used for communication?

❏ Do you use examples with specific details to illustrate the advantages and disadvantages?

❏ Do you have paragraph unity? Do all the sentences support the topic sentence?

❏ Are gerunds and infinitives used correctly?

❏ Are commas and colons used correctly?

UNIT 6

Woman's Work?

OVERVIEW	
Theme:	Male and female roles
Prewriting:	Freewriting
Organizing:	Supporting an opinion
Revising:	Writing concluding sentences
	Using adverbs of frequency
Editing:	Correcting sentence fragments

Assignment

In Unit 6 of *NorthStar: Reading and Writing,* Second Edition, you read about men, women, and housework. Who do you think should do the housework in a family? The assignment for this unit is to read and discuss some quotations about the work men and women do around the house. You will write a paragraph expressing your opinion about one of these quotations.

1 Prewriting

FREEWRITING

 Complete Unit 6, Sections 1–3, in the Student Book before you begin this section.

Freewriting can help you to think of your ideas before you write your paragraph. When you freewrite, you write for a short period of time without stopping. You quickly write down all your ideas about your topic without thinking about organization, grammar, or spelling. Later, you use your ideas to write your first draft.

For this assignment, you will freewrite your opinion about a quotation about men, women, and housework.

1 *Work in a group. Read each quotation about men, women, and housework. Then choose the statement that best gives the meaning of the quotation.*

1. "Little boys, little girls
when you're big husbands and wives,
if you want all of the days of your lives to seem sunny as summer weather,
make sure when there's housework to do that you do it together."

—Sheldon Harnick ("Housework")

What does this quotation mean?

   a. Husbands and wives should do housework when it is sunny outside.
   b. Little boys and girls should do housework together.
   c. To be happy, husbands and wives should do housework together.

2. "A man works from sun to sun, but a woman's work is never done."

—Proverb

What does this quotation mean?

   a. Men like to work in the sun, but women don't.
   b. Men stop working when the sun goes down, but women do housework all the time.
   c. Men finish their work on time, but women are always late.

2 *In your group, answer the following questions about each quotation you read.*

1. What does the writer think about men, women, and housework? Who should do the housework? Who works more every day? Explain your answer.

2. Do you agree or disagree with the writer? Give some reasons or examples to support your opinion.

3 *Choose one of the quotations in this section that you would like to write about. On a separate piece of paper, freewrite about the quotation for at least five minutes without stopping. Don't worry about grammar. Just try to make your ideas clear. Use the following questions to help you.*

- What quotation are you writing about?

- What does it mean?

- What's your opinion? Do you agree or disagree with the writer?

- What examples can you give to support your opinion?

2 Organizing

SUPPORTING AN OPINION

In your paragraph, you need to explain why you agree or disagree with the quotation. To support your opinion, you can make general statements and give specific examples.

- A general statement is something that you think is true for everyone.

  Men and women both work hard.

- A specific example is something from your experience or the experience of someone you know.

  My father and mother both work full time. Then they come home and do all the housework.

The general statement can be part of the topic sentence. The rest of the paragraph can explain the topic sentence with specific examples.

1 *Read the example paragraph and complete the tasks below.*

"Marrying is easy; it's housework that's hard."   —Proverb

I agree with this proverb because married couples often have different opinions about housework. For example, my husband and I disagree about doing housework. He has a full-time job, so he is tired when he gets home. He doesn't want to do much housework. Sometimes he cooks dinner or does the laundry, but usually he wants to relax. He thinks I should do most of the housework. However, I have a part-time job, and I take care of the children after school. I'm also very tired in the evening. I think my husband should help me more with the cooking and cleaning. Housework is the only thing we argue about. Housework can make marriage difficult.

1. Underline the topic sentence that states the writer's opinion about the quotation.
2. Circle the general statement in the topic sentence.
3. What example does the writer use to support her opinion?

2 *Read the statements. Write **G** next to the general statements and **S** next to the specific examples.*

_____ **1.** Each child in my family has a different job around the house, such as cleaning the kitchen or taking out the garbage.

_____ **2.** Housework should be shared by all the members of a family.

_____ **3.** Men and women have different responsibilities in a marriage.

_____ **4.** My family pays a housekeeper to come once a week to clean the house.

_____ **5.** My father earns money for our family, and my mother takes care of the house.

_____ **6.** You can pay someone to do your housework.

3 *Match the general statements above with the specific examples that support them. Write the number of the general statement and its supporting example in the spaces.*

General statement _____ is supported by example _____.

General statement _____ is supported by example _____.

General statement _____ is supported by example _____.

4 *Look at your freewriting from Exercise 3 on page 40. Underline the examples that support your opinion. Are they specific enough? Do you write about your own experience or that of someone you know? Add specific examples where they are needed.*

WRITING THE FIRST DRAFT

Use the information from the previous sections to write the first draft of your paragraph.

- Write the quotation and the name of the person who said it at the top of the page.

- Write a topic sentence stating your opinion about the quotation. For example, you can write: "I agree with this quotation by Sheldon Harnick because . . ." or "I disagree with this proverb because . . ." Make a general statement to explain your opinion about the quotation.

- In the rest of the paragraph, give specific examples to support the general statement.

Don't worry too much about grammar. Just try to make your ideas clear.

PEER REVIEW

When you finish your first draft, exchange papers with another student. Read your partner's first draft and answer the questions below. Then discuss your answers with your partner.

- What is the writer's opinion about the quotation?
- What general statement does the writer make to explain his or her opinion?
- What specific examples does the writer use to support the general statement?
- Which examples are most effective? Why?

Discuss your partner's reaction to your paragraph. Make a note of any parts you need to revise.

3 Revising

A WRITING CONCLUDING SENTENCES

The concluding sentence is the last sentence in your paragraph. It brings your paragraph to an end. A concluding sentence can restate the main idea of the paragraph or add the writer's final thoughts about the topic.

1 *Read the example paragraph on page 41 again. Underline the concluding sentence in the paragraph. Does it restate the writer's main idea from the topic sentence?*

2 *Read the topic sentences. Match them with the appropriate concluding sentences.*

Topic Sentences

_____ 1. I agree with this proverb because women usually have to do all the housework.

_____ 2. I disagree with this proverb because men and women both have to work hard these days.

_____ 3. I disagree with this quotation because men and women should have different responsibilities in a family.

_____ 4. I agree with this quotation because it is more fun to work together.

Concluding Sentences

a. Men and women both are very busy at work and at home.

b. Men should work to earn money and women should take care of the house and children.

c. Men and women can enjoy doing housework together instead of fighting about it.

d. Women do much more work around the house than men do.

3 *Look at your first draft. Write a concluding sentence that restates the main idea of your topic sentence or adds a final thought about the topic.*

B USING ADVERBS OF FREQUENCY

 Complete Unit 6, Section 4B, in the Student Book before you begin this section.

Adverbs of frequency describe how often someone does something.

1 *Add an adverb of frequency from the box to each statement. Each statement should explain your opinion about the work you think men and women do. You can use each adverb more than one time.*

always	usually	often
sometimes	rarely	never

1. Men and women share the housework.

2. Men do the cooking.

3. Women enjoy doing housework.

4. Taking care of children is an easy job.

5. Women take care of the children.

2 *Compare your sentences with a partner's sentences. Did you use the adverbs correctly? Do you agree with your partner's statements?*

3 *Look at your first draft. Did you use any adverbs of frequency? If you did, are they used correctly? If you did not, find two or three places where you can add adverbs of frequency.*

WRITING THE SECOND DRAFT

Now you are ready to write your second draft. Look at all your notes from the previous sections to help you revise.

• Write a concluding sentence for your paragraph.

• Use adverbs of frequency to describe how often things happen.

4 Editing

CORRECTING SENTENCE FRAGMENTS

A sentence fragment is an incomplete sentence. There are different reasons for sentence fragments:

- The subject is missing. To correct the problem, add a subject.

                                                            sentence fragment

  Incorrect: *My dad helps with the housework.* <u>*Sometimes cooks dinner.*</u>

  Correct: *My dad helps with the housework.* <u>*He sometimes cooks dinner.*</u>

- Part of a sentence is used as a complete sentence. To correct the problem, combine the parts into one sentence.

                                        sentence fragment

  Incorrect: *I don't like to cook.* <u>*Or do the laundry.*</u>

  Correct: *I don't like to cook* <u>*or do the laundry.*</u>

1 *Underline the sentence fragments. Then correct them. Write the corrected sentences on the lines.*

1. Many men work full time. And around the house.

   _____

2. I work harder than my husband. Cook, clean, and go to my job every day.

   _____

3. My mother and father share the housework. Work together to cook and clean.

   _____

4. Men work harder than women. And earn more money.

   _____

2 *Look at your second draft. Correct any sentence fragments.*

PREPARING THE FINAL DRAFT

Carefully edit your second draft. Use the checklist below as a guide. Then neatly write or type your paragraph with the corrections.

> **FINAL DRAFT CHECKLIST**
>
> ❏ Is your quotation given at the top of the page?
>
> ❏ Does your topic sentence state your opinion and make a general statement about the reason for your opinion?
>
> ❏ Does your paragraph include specific examples to support your opinion?
>
> ❏ Is there a concluding sentence that restates the main idea of the paragraph or adds a final thought?
>
> ❏ Are adverbs of frequency used correctly?
>
> ❏ Did you correct all the sentence fragments?

Organic Produce: Is It Worth the Price?

OVERVIEW	
Theme:	Food
Prewriting:	Clustering
Organizing:	Writing for your audience
Revising:	Choosing descriptive adjectives
	Using count and non-count nouns
Editing:	Correcting run-on sentences

Assignment

In Unit 7 of *Northstar: Reading and Writing,* Second Edition, you read about organic food. What kind of food do you like? The assignment for this unit is to write a restaurant review. You will describe the restaurant and the food it serves.

1 Prewriting

CLUSTERING

Complete Unit 7, Sections 1–3, in the Student Book before you begin this section.

Restaurant reviews help people choose restaurants. They tell the reader about the food, prices, location, service (how the waiters treat the customers), and atmosphere (the feeling) of a restaurant.

One way to get ideas for your restaurant review is clustering. Clustering helps you see your ideas and how they are connected. In a cluster diagram, the main idea is in a large circle in the middle. New ideas are in smaller circles and are all connected to the main idea.

1 *Look at the cluster diagram for a restaurant called the Stinking Rose. The writer has made a cluster diagram about the food, prices, location, service, and atmosphere of the restaurant.*

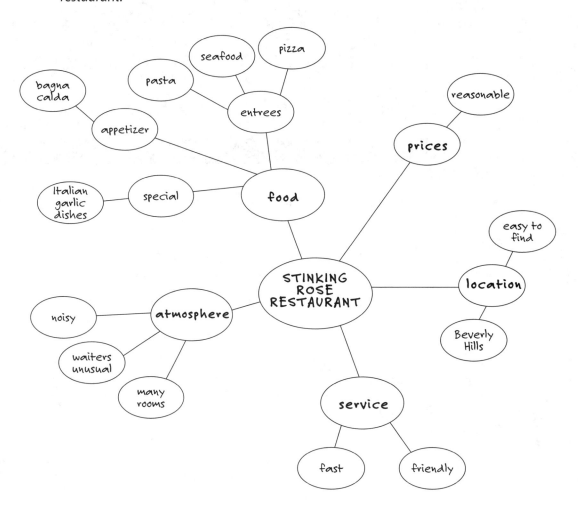

2 *Choose a restaurant to write about. It can be one you like or don't like. Make a cluster diagram for the restaurant. Start with a large circle in the middle of the paper. Write the name of the restaurant in the circle. What information do you want to include in your review? Write ideas in smaller circles and connect them to the middle circle. Use these ideas or some of your own.*

Food
Location
Atmosphere
Prices
Service

Continue writing ideas and connecting them to the circles. You don't have to use all the ideas in your review.

2 Organizing

WRITING FOR YOUR AUDIENCE

Complete Unit 7, Section 4A, in the Student Book before you begin this section.

The people who read your writing are your audience. Think about your audience when you are deciding what to include in your restaurant review. Different audiences are interested in different kinds of information.

1 *Imagine that you are writing two restaurant reviews, one for a student newspaper and one for a magazine for gourmet cooks (people who love to cook and eat fancy food). What type of information should you include in each review? Read the list below. Is the information important to the students, the gourmet cooks, or both? Put a check (✓) in the appropriate column. When you are done, discuss your answers.*

	Students	Cooks	Both
1. The restaurant is located near a bus stop.	❏	❏	❏
2. The chef studied in France.	❏	❏	❏
3. The restaurant accepts credit cards.	❏	❏	❏
4. You can buy cooking products at the restaurant.	❏	❏	❏
5. The food is not expensive.	❏	❏	❏
6. You can go with a large group of friends.	❏	❏	❏
7. Many of the ingredients are organic.	❏	❏	❏
8. The restaurant has a five-star rating.	❏	❏	❏

2 *Read these six excerpts from a review of the Stinking Rose. Which three pieces of information would you include for an audience of students? Which three would you include for an audience of gourmet cooks? Write **S** for students and **C** for cooks.*

_____ 1. You can purchase cooking products from the restaurant. They sell tools for preparing and cooking garlic. They also sell a cookbook with their most popular recipes.

_____ 2. The prices are not too high. Appetizers cost from $5 to $7, and main dishes are under $12. The servings are large, so you always get enough to eat.

_____ 3. The restaurant is easy to get to by car or bus. It is located near a bus stop. There is free parking across the street.

_____ 4. The food is Italian, and all the dishes are made with garlic. One famous dish is called *bagna calda*. It is made of garlic cloves roasted in olive oil and butter. The restaurant also serves several different pizzas, all with lots of garlic. They also have pasta and seafood dishes. For dessert, you can order garlic ice cream!

_____ 5. The chef at the Stinking Rose is world famous for his garlic recipes. He studied traditional French cooking in France. When he came to California, he worked at many famous restaurants. He opened the Stinking Rose ten years ago. He teaches at the California Cooking Academy.

_____ 6. The restaurant is informal. There are three dining rooms. They are decorated with many pictures of garlic. The service is excellent. The waiters are very friendly and fast. You don't have to wait a long time for your food.

3 *After you choose the information for your review, you must decide how to organize it. One way to organize your ideas is by order of importance—putting the most important information first. Read the topic sentence for the student newspaper and the topic sentence for the gourmet magazine below. Put the information you chose in order of importance for each review. Write the numbers on the lines. The first one is the most important.*

Student Newspaper

The Stinking Rose is a great restaurant for students.

a. _____

b. _____

c. _____

Gourmet Magazine

The Stinking Rose is a great restaurant for garlic lovers.

a. _____

b. _____

c. _____

WRITING THE FIRST DRAFT

Use the information from the previous sections to write the first draft of your review.

- Choose an audience for your review. The audience can be students, gourmet cooks, or another group.

- Start your review with a topic sentence that includes the name of the restaurant.

- Choose the information to include in your review. Make sure the information is important to the audience.

- Put the information in order of importance. Write several sentences for each part of the review.

Don't worry too much about grammar. Just try to make your ideas clear.

PEER REVIEW

When you finish your first draft, exchange papers with another student. Read your partner's first draft and answer the questions below. Then discuss your answers with your partner.

- What is the name of the restaurant?

- Who is the audience for this review? How can you tell?

- What type of information is included in the review? Is it appropriate for the audience?

- Is the information in order of importance?

- Do you think any important information was left out? If so, what?

Discuss your partner's reaction to your review. Make a note of any parts you need to revise.

---

3 Revising

A CHOOSING DESCRIPTIVE ADJECTIVES

There are many adjectives you can use to describe a restaurant and the food it serves. Using adjectives will make your writing more interesting and descriptive.

1 *Match the adjectives with their meanings. If necessary, use a dictionary to help you.*

**Adjectives to describe
the taste of food**

Meanings

_____ 1. bland   a. with sugar

_____ 2. fresh   b. with salt

_____ 3. greasy   c. with hot chili pepper

_____ 4. juicy   d. with a lot of butter and cream

_____ 5. rich   e. without much flavor

_____ 6. salty   f. not old

_____ 7. spicy   g. with a lot of oil

_____ 8. sweet   h. not dry, full of juice

2 *Choose adjectives from Exercise 1. Make sentences with the adjectives to describe the following dishes. Then write a descriptive sentence about one of the dishes in your review.*

French fries: *French fries are salty and greasy.*

Chocolate ice cream: _____

Organic tomatoes: _____

From your review:

_____   _____

3 *Match the adjectives with their meanings. If necessary, use a dictionary to help you.*

**Adjectives to describe
a restaurant**

Meanings

_____ 1. casual   a. fashionable

_____ 2. cozy   b. formal, of high quality

_____ 3. crowded   c. not formal

_____ 4. fancy   d. too expensive

_____ 5. old-fashioned   e. full of too many people

_____ 6. overpriced   f. not modern or new

_____ 7. reasonable   g. small and friendly

_____ 8. trendy   h. not priced too high

4 *Choose adjectives from Exercise 3 to describe the following types of restaurants. Make sentences with the adjectives. Then write a descriptive sentence about the restaurant you are reviewing.*

Fast-food restaurants: _____

Gourmet restaurants: _____

Your restaurant:

_____   _____

5 *Look at your first draft. Add more description of the food and the restaurant using some of the adjectives in this section.*

B USING COUNT AND NON-COUNT NOUNS

Complete Unit 7, Section 4B, in the Student Book before you begin this section.

1 *Each one of the following sentences has a mistake in count and non-count nouns. Correct the mistakes.*

               a
1. The Stinking Rose is famous restaurant in Beverly Hills.
           ^

2. *Bagna calda* is made from garlic cloves roasted in olive oils and butter.

3. It is served with breads.

4. The desserts don't have some garlic in them.

5. They serve lot of delicious food.

6. They sell a tools for preparing and cooking garlic.

7. The chef has worked at any famous restaurants.

8. The Stinking Rose is interesting restaurant.

2 *Look at your restaurant review. Did you use count and non-count nouns correctly? Correct any mistakes.*

WRITING THE SECOND DRAFT

Now you are ready to write your second draft. Look at all your notes from the previous sections to help you revise.

- Use specific adjectives to describe the atmosphere of the restaurant and the food.

- Use count and non-count nouns correctly.

4 Editing

CORRECTING RUN-ON SENTENCES

A run-on sentence occurs when two sentences are put together with no punctuation between them. To correct run-on sentences, add a period between the two sentences. Make sure each of the sentences has a subject and a verb.

Incorrect: *There are also several pasta dishes one is neon ravioli.*

Correct: *There are also several pasta dishes. One is neon ravioli.*

1 *Correct the run-on sentences.*

1. Some of their famous dishes include *bagna calda*, which is garlic cloves roasted in olive oil and butter it's served with bread.

2. I tried the neon ravioli, which is filled with cheese and garlic there are also seafood dishes including a delicious baked salmon with garlic.

3. Prices are reasonable appetizers are from $6.00 to $9.50 entrées are from $10.50 to $15.00.

4. Service is excellent it is very fast.

2 *Look at your second draft. Find any run-on sentences and correct them.*

PREPARING THE FINAL DRAFT

Carefully edit your second draft. Use the checklist below as a guide. Then neatly write or type your paragraph with the corrections.

FINAL DRAFT CHECKLIST

- ❏ Did you choose a specific audience for the restaurant review?
- ❏ Does the paragraph have a topic sentence that names the restaurant you are reviewing?
- ❏ Do you include information in the review that is important to your audience?
- ❏ Is the information in order of importance?
- ❏ Do you use specific adjectives to describe the restaurant and its food?
- ❏ Are the count and non-count nouns used correctly?
- ❏ Did you correct the run-on sentences?

8

"I'll take the train, thanks."

OVERVIEW	
Theme:	Travel
Prewriting:	Charting
Organizing:	Outlining
Revising:	Connecting ideas with *and* and *but*
	Expressing ability and possibility with *can* and *can't*
Editing:	Punctuating sentences with *and* and *but*

Assignment

In Unit 8 of *NorthStar: Reading and Writing,* Second Edition, you read about traveling from London to Kyoto by train, ferry, and bicycle. How do you like to travel? The assignment for this unit is to write two paragraphs describing the best and worst ways to travel to a particular place. You will explain the advantages and disadvantages of each way to travel.

1 Prewriting

CHARTING

 Complete Unit 8, Sections 1–3, in the Student Book before you begin this section.

There are many ways to travel—by plane, train, or bus. Each way has advantages and disadvantages. Making a chart can help you focus on the advantages and disadvantages.

1 *Look at the chart about four ways to get from San Francisco, California, to Los Angeles, California. Look at the advantages and disadvantages for each one.*

From San Francisco to Los Angeles

WAYS TO TRAVEL	ADVANTAGES	DISADVANTAGES
Plane	convenient fast	often late expensive at popular travel times crowded, uncomfortable makes more pollution
Train	nice scenery relaxing low pollution	slow expensive
Car	go when you want stop anywhere, anytime	traffic tiring
Bus	inexpensive can get off to see things	slow, many stops uncomfortable, crowded makes more pollution

2 *Think about different places you have traveled. Pick one trip to write about. It can be a short trip, such as going across town, or a long trip, such as going to another country. Then think of three or four different ways to make the trip, such as flying, walking, riding a bicycle, or taking the train. Make a chart showing the advantages and disadvantages of the different ways to travel.*

3 *Look at your chart. Choose the best way and the worst way to go on the trip.*

2 Organizing

OUTLINING

Outlining shows the order of main points and details. Look at the outline for two paragraphs on the best and worst ways to travel on page 58.

Outline: Best way and worst way to travel

I. Best way to travel

    A. Advantages

        1. Detail 1: Explain one advantage

        2. Detail 2: Explain another advantage

    B. Disadvantages

        1. Detail 1: Explain a disadvantage

II. Worst way to travel

    A. Disadvantages

        1. Detail 1: Explain one disadvantage

        2. Detail 2: Explain another disadvantage

    B. Advantages

        1. Detail 1: Explain an advantage

1 *Read the paragraphs. Then complete the outline on page 59 with the missing details from the paragraphs.*

Traveling from San Francisco to Los Angeles

The best way to travel from San Francisco to Los Angeles is to take a plane. There are many advantages to flying. One advantage is that flying is fast. It takes about an hour to fly from San Francisco to Los Angeles, and the flight is nonstop. Another advantage is that flying is convenient. There are three airports near San Francisco. You can get to the airports by driving, going on the subway, or taking a shuttle bus. However, flying has disadvantages too. Sometimes flying is stressful. Planes are often late, and you have to go through a lot of security checks at the airport. Overall, flying is fast and convenient, but it is sometimes stressful.

Going by bus is the worst way to travel from San Francisco to Los Angeles. There are several disadvantages. One disadvantage is that buses are very slow. The trip takes more than eight hours, and the bus makes many stops. Sometimes you have to wait a long time during the stops. Another disadvantage is that buses are uncomfortable. The seats are small and hard, and the bus is often crowded. However, traveling by bus has advantages too. One advantage is that your schedule is very flexible. You can stop and visit towns along the way. You can also change the date or time of your ticket easily. In conclusion, traveling by bus is slow and uncomfortable, but the schedule is flexible.

Outline: Traveling from San Francisco to Los Angeles

I. Topic sentence: Flying is best way to travel to Los Angeles.

    A. Advantages

        1. Fast

            a. One hour to L.A.

            b. _____

        2. Convenient

            a. Three airports: San Francisco, Oakland, or San Jose

            b. _____

    B. Disadvantages

        1. Stressful

            a. _____

            b. Many security checks

II. Topic sentence: The worst way to travel to Los Angeles is to take a bus.

    A. Disadvantages

        1. Slow

            a. _____

            b. Makes many stops

        2. Uncomfortable

            a. _____

            b. Crowded

    B. Advantages

        1. Flexible schedule

            a. _____

            b. Can change date or time of ticket easily

2 *Make an outline for your paragraphs. Use the ideas from the chart you made in Exercise 2 on page 57.*

- Choose the best and worst way to travel to a place.

- Look at the advantages and disadvantages in the chart. Choose the most important ones to include in your paragraphs.

- Think of details to explain the advantages and disadvantages.

WRITING THE FIRST DRAFT

Use the information from the previous sections to write the first draft of your paragraphs.

- Write a topic sentence for each of your paragraphs.

- Organize your paragraphs according to the outline you wrote.

- Include supporting ideas and details.

- Write a concluding sentence for each paragraph. The concluding sentence can summarize your opinion about the type of travel. For example, "Flying is convenient and fast, but it can be stressful."

Don't worry too much about grammar. Just try to make your ideas clear.

PEER REVIEW

When you finish your first draft, exchange papers with another student. Read your partner's first draft and answer the questions below. Then discuss your answers with your partner.

- Which two types of transportation does the writer describe? Between what two places?

- Does the writer describe the advantages and disadvantages of both types of transportation?

- What details and examples does the writer use to explain the advantages and disadvantages? Which details are most effective? Which details can be improved?

Discuss your partner's reaction to your first draft. Make a note of any parts you need to revise.

3 Revising

A CONNECTING IDEAS WITH *AND* AND *BUT*

 Complete Unit 8, Section 4A, in the Student Book before you begin this section.

Good writing has a variety of sentence types. One way to have sentence variety is to use the sentence connectors *and* and *but*. **And** connects similar ideas in the same sentence. **But** connects contrasting ideas in the same sentence.

1 *Combine the sentences with* **and** *or* **but.**

   1. The drive to Los Angeles is very long. Sometimes there is a lot of traffic.

   _____

   2. Buying gas to drive to Los Angeles is expensive. Airline tickets are more expensive.

   _____

   3. You need a car to get around in Los Angeles. You need a car to take trips outside the city.

   _____

   4. Taking the train to Los Angeles is relaxing and enjoyable. It is slow.

   _____

   5. You can buy snacks on the train. You can't watch a movie.

   _____

   6. You can look out the window. You can talk to people.

   _____

2 *Look at your first draft. Did you use* **and** *and* **but** *to connect your ideas? If you did, are they used correctly? If you did not, rewrite sentences that you can connect with* **and** *or* **but.**

B EXPRESSING ABILITY AND POSSIBILITY WITH *CAN* AND *CAN'T*

Complete Unit 8, Section 4B, in the Student Book before you begin this section.

Can and *can't* express ability or possibility in the present. You can use *can* and *can't* to suggest different possibilities for traveling.

1 *Read about three ways of traveling from San Francisco to Los Angeles. Decide what is possible with each type of travel and what is not possible. Then write sentences using* **can** *and* **can't.**

1. Taking a train

   a. See the coast

   You can see the beautiful California coast from the train.

   b. Relax

   _____

   c. Be in a hurry

   _____

2. Driving

   a. Make your own schedule

   _____

   b. Stop when you want

   _____

   c. Sleep while you travel

   _____

3. Riding a bicycle

   a. Help reduce pollution

   _____

   b. Get some exercise

   _____

   c. Stop and look at things along the way

   _____

2 *Look at your first draft. Did you use* **can** *and* **can't** *to describe possibilities? If you did, are they used correctly? If you did not, find one or two places where you can add a sentence with* **can** *or* **can't.**

WRITING THE SECOND DRAFT

Now you are ready to write your second draft. Look at all your notes from the previous sections to help you revise.

- Connect sentences with *and* or *but* to describe advantages or disadvantages. Don't repeat the subject after using *and* or *but*.

- Use *can* or *can't* to talk about abilities or possibilities.

4 Editing

PUNCTUATING SENTENCES WITH *AND* AND *BUT*

When you connect two sentences with *and* or *but*, use a comma between the two ideas.

*The flight to Los Angeles is fast, **and** it is nonstop.*

1 *Add commas to the sentences.*

1. You can relax on the train and you don't have to look at a map for directions.

2. The train is slower than flying but you can see the beautiful scenery along the way.

3. The bus is cheap but it makes a lot of stops. In addition, it is often crowded and it can be very uncomfortable.

4. Flying is the fastest but it can cost the most. You can find cheap tickets but tickets are more expensive during popular travel times.

5. Riding a bicycle is a good way to help reduce air pollution and you can get some exercise.

2 *Look at your second draft. Have you used commas correctly with **and** and **but**? Make any necessary corrections.*

PREPARING THE FINAL DRAFT

Carefully edit your second draft. Use the checklist below as a guide. Then neatly write or type your paragraphs with the corrections.

FINAL DRAFT CHECKLIST

❏ Do you have two paragraphs describing the best and worst way to travel to a place?

❏ Do you include details to explain the advantages and disadvantages of each type of travel?

❏ Do you connect your ideas with *and* and *but*?

❏ Do you use *can* and *can't* to describe ability and possibility?

❏ Do you use commas correctly with *and* and *but*?

The Winter Blues

OVERVIEW	
Theme:	Health
Prewriting:	Describing pictures
Organizing:	Describing a process
Revising:	Adding descriptive details using nouns and adjectives
	Using *should* and *shouldn't* for advice
Editing:	Punctuating direct speech

Assignment

In Unit 9 of *NorthStar: Reading and Writing,* Second Edition, you read about SAD (Seasonal Affective Disorder) and different ways to treat it. What are some other ways to treat health problems? The assignment for this unit is to think of another health problem and invent your own health product to treat it. You will draw a picture of the product and write an advertisement describing it and telling how to use it.

1 Prewriting

DESCRIBING PICTURES

Complete Unit 9, Sections 1–3, in the Student Book before you begin this section.

Drawing pictures can help you to think of details about your health product and how to use it.

1 *Work with a partner. Look at the pictures and answer these questions:*

1. What is the man doing in each picture?

2. How does he feel?

3. What is the health treatment he's using?

4. How do you think it works?

Before   **After**

2 *Look at the pictures again. Write the descriptions from the box on the correct lines.*

- It tastes sweet and delicious; it smells like oranges and lemons.
- All-natural tea and herbs
- "It's terrific! It really works! I lost weight and now I feel great!"
- Put it in boiling water. Drink it two times a day until you lose all the weight you want.
- Thin-Fast Diet Tea
- He's overweight.
- It helps you to lose weight, even when you eat a lot.

The man's problem: _____

Product name: _____

What the product does: _____

What it's made of: _____

What it's like (description): _____

How you use it: _____

Comment from a happy customer: _____

3 *Answer the following questions and draw some pictures to help you think of details about your own product. Don't worry about how good your drawings are. Just try to include the information you need.*

1. On a separate sheet of paper, draw a picture of a person who needs this product.

2. What health problem does your product treat? _____

3. What's the name of the product? _____

4. What does it do? _____

5. Describe your product. What does it look, smell, taste, or feel like? What is it made of? _____

_____

6. How do you use the product? _____

_____

7. What does the customer think about the product? _____

_____

8. On a separate sheet of paper, draw a picture of a person using the product.

2 Organizing

DESCRIBING A PROCESS

In your ad, you will need to explain the process of using your product. When you describe a process, you describe things in time order—what to do first, second, third, and so on.

1 *Read the following sentences. Number the sentences in the correct order, from **1** to **4**.*

_____ Thin-Fast is fast and easy to use.

_____ Continue to drink Thin-Fast until you lose all the weight you want. In the end, you'll look and feel great.

_____ First, boil some water.

_____ Then put the Thin-Fast Diet Tea in the water for five minutes.

2 *Now write sentences to explain how to use your product. Write the process in the correct order.*

1. _____

2. _____

3. _____

4. _____

5. _____

WRITING THE FIRST DRAFT

Use the information from the previous sections to write the first draft of your ad.

In the first paragraph:

- Give the name of the health product and explain what it can do.

- Describe the health product. What does it look, smell, taste, or feel like?

In the second paragraph:

- Explain how to use the health product.

- Give a comment from a happy customer.

PEER REVIEW

When you finish your draft, exchange papers with another student. Read your partner's first draft and answer the questions below. Then discuss your answers with your partner.

- Does the writer give the name of the product and describe it? Is there any more information you would like to know about the product?

- Does the writer explain how to use the product? Are there any steps missing? Are all the steps clear? If not, underline the parts that are not clear.

- Does the writer include a comment from a customer?

- Is the ad convincing? (Does it make you want to buy the product?) If not, what could the writer say to make the ad more convincing?

Discuss your partner's reaction to your advertisement. Make a note of any parts you need to revise.

3 Revising

A ADDING DESCRIPTIVE DETAILS USING NOUNS AND ADJECTIVES

Details about the color, size, shape, smell, taste, and feel of your health product are important. Here are some ways you can talk about these descriptive details:

$$ \text{It} \begin{bmatrix} \text{is} \\ \text{looks} \\ \text{smells} \\ \text{feels} \\ \text{tastes} \end{bmatrix} + \textbf{adjective} \qquad \text{It} \begin{bmatrix} \text{is} \\ \text{looks} \\ \text{smells} \\ \text{feels} \\ \text{tastes} \end{bmatrix} + like + \textbf{noun} $$

Examples

It smells delicious.

It tastes delicious.

It smells like lemons.

It tastes like lemons.

1 *Use the adjectives and nouns below to write descriptive sentences with* **is, looks, smells, tastes,** *and* **feels.**

Example

soft and smooth _It feels soft and smooth._

1. chocolate _____

2. fast and easy to use _____

3. spring flowers _____

4. a tiny pill _____

5. convenient _____

6. terrific _____

2 *Look at the first draft of your ad. Where appropriate, add descriptive details with nouns and adjectives.*

B   USING *SHOULD* AND *SHOULDN'T* FOR ADVICE

Complete Unit 9, Section 4B, in the Student Book before you begin this section.

In your ad, you need to give advice about using your health product. To give advice, use *should* and *shouldn't*.

1 *Read the ad for Thin-Fast Diet Tea. Rewrite the underlined sentences using* **should** *or* **shouldn't**.

Thin-Fast Diet Tea is a fantastic new weight-loss product. It helps you to lose weight quickly. It's made of all-natural herbs and plants, so it's safe to use. It smells like lemons and oranges, and it tastes sweet and delicious.

Thin-Fast is fast and easy to use. First, boil some water. Then put the Thin-Fast Diet Tea in the water for five minutes. (**1**) Drink Thin-Fast twice a day, once in the morning and once in the evening. (**2**) Continue to drink Thin-Fast every day until you lose all the weight you want. In the end, you'll look and feel great. This happy customer says, "Thin-Fast is terrific! It really works! I lost 65 pounds in only three months. Now I feel thin, happy, and full of energy. (**3**) Don't spend another day dieting and exercising. You can eat all the food you want and still lose weight with Thin-Fast. (**4**) Buy some today!"

1. _____

2. _____

3. _____

4. _____

2 *Look at the first draft of your ad. Did you use* should *and* shouldn't *to give advice? Underline some sentences where you can use* should *and* shouldn't *and write some new sentences to put in your ad.*

WRITING THE SECOND DRAFT

Now you are ready to write your second draft. Look at your notes from the previous sections to help you revise.

• Use nouns and adjectives to describe your health product in detail.

• Use *should* and *shouldn't* to give advice about using your health product.

4 | Editing

PUNCTUATING DIRECT SPEECH

Complete Unit 9, Section 4A, in the Student Book before you begin this section.

1 *Read the following sentences and correct the punctuation errors for direct speech.*

1. One customer said "Thin-Fast changed my life!"

2. I feel happy and full of energy, Mary Ann said.

3. Customers who use Thin-Fast say, "It's terrific!" "It really works!"

4. I asked "What do you think of Thin-Fast?"

2 *Look at the quote from a happy customer in your second draft. Correct any errors in using direct speech.*

PREPARING THE FINAL DRAFT

Carefully edit your second draft. Use the checklist below as a guide. Then neatly write or type your ad with the corrections.

FINAL DRAFT CHECKLIST

❏ Do you give the name of the health product and explain what it can do?

❏ Do you use nouns and adjectives to describe the health product?

❏ Do you explain how to use the health product?

❏ Do you include a comment from a happy customer and use direct speech correctly?

❏ Do you use *should* and *shouldn't* to give advice about using your health product?

UNIT 10

Endangered Cultures

OVERVIEW

Theme:	Endangered cultures
Prewriting:	Using information from a reading
Organizing:	Outlining
Revising:	Writing a concluding sentence
	Expressing future predictions with *will* and *be going to*
Editing:	Correcting verb forms

Assignment

In Unit 10 of *NorthStar: Reading and Writing,* Second Edition, you read about endangered cultures. How can you tell which cultures and languages will disappear and which will survive? The assignment for this unit is to read about four endangered languages. You will use the information to write two paragraphs predicting what will happen to two of the languages.

1 Prewriting

USING INFORMATION FROM A READING

 Complete Unit 10, Sections 1–3, in the Student Book before you begin this section.

Before you write about certain topics, you need to read about them. So it's important to know how to use the information from a reading.

1 *Read the information in these FAQs (frequently asked questions) about some endangered languages. As you read, think about whether or not these languages will survive in the future.*

FAQs: Endangered Languages

KARITIANA

Where is Karitiana spoken?
Karitiana is spoken in the small town of Porto Velho, Brazil. Portuguese is spoken in other parts of Brazil.

How many people speak Karitiana?
Only 185 people speak Karitiana. The total population of Porto Velho is 191.

How do people learn Karitiana?
Families speak Karitiana at home. Children learn Karitiana and Portuguese at school.

How is Karitiana used in everyday life?
Karitiana is spoken only in Porto Velho. People must speak Portuguese if they go to other parts of the country.

What is being done to preserve the Karitiana language?
Linguists are writing down the grammar and making a dictionary. People are writing down traditional stories.

SCOTTISH GAELIC

Where is Scottish Gaelic spoken?
Scottish Gaelic is spoken on the Western Isles of Scotland.

How many people speak Scottish Gaelic?
About 70,000 people speak Scottish Gaelic. The total population of these islands is 88,000.

How do people learn Scottish Gaelic?
Many children learn Gaelic at home, and there are Gaelic-language playgroups and schools. Adults can also learn Gaelic. For example, a college on the Isle of Skye teaches the Scottish Gaelic language, music, and culture. Universities in Scotland, England, Canada, and the United States also teach Scottish Gaelic.

How is Scottish Gaelic used in everyday life?
Gaelic is used in many stores and businesses. There are newspapers, radio shows, and TV programs in Scottish Gaelic.

What is being done to preserve the Scottish Gaelic language?
There is information about Gaelic on the Internet, including online dictionaries, language courses, and mailing lists. People around the world can join organizations to meet other Gaelic speakers.

POTAWATOMI

Where is Potawatomi spoken?
Potawatomi is spoken on Walpole Island in Ontario, Canada, and also in Michigan, Wisconsin, Kansas, and Oklahoma in the United States.

How many people speak Potawatomi?
There are fewer than 50 fluent speakers. Most speakers are middle-aged or older.

How do people learn Potawatomi?
Most children do not learn Potawatomi at home. There are some preschool programs that teach Potawatomi.

How is Potawatomi used in everyday life?
Potawatomi speakers must use English in business, education, and government.

What is being done to preserve the Potawatomi language?
There is one Potawatomi dictionary. Linguists are studying the grammar and making videotapes of fluent Potawatomi speakers. There are several Web sites with information about the Potawatomi language. *(continued)*

MAORI

Where is Maori spoken?
Maori is spoken in New Zealand.
How many people speak Maori?
There are 50,000 to 70,000 Maori speakers; 71
percent are over 45 years old. The total Maori
population is more than 310,000.
How do people learn Maori?
The government pays for language programs
in the schools. There are also classes that
teach Maori to adults.

How is Maori used in everyday life?
There are TV shows in Maori for children and
adults. Maori is also spoken during religious
activities.
**Is anything being done to preserve
the Maori language?**
Maori is now an official language in New
Zealand. A governmental group called the
Maori Language Commission works to make
sure the Maori language survives. They try to
encourage the use of Maori.

2 *Work in a small group to complete the chart below. Decide which language you think
will survive and which won't. Use the information in the FAQs to give details to support
your opinion about the language.*

LANGUAGE	PREDICTION (check one)	SUPPORTING DETAILS
Karitiana	❏ will survive ❏ won't survive	• only 185 speakers • can't use it in other places • _____ • _____
Scottish Gaelic	❏ will survive ❏ won't survive	• _____ • _____ • _____ • _____
Potawatomi	❏ will survive ❏ won't survive	• _____ • _____ • _____ • _____
Maori	❏ will survive ❏ won't survive	• _____ • _____ • _____ • _____

2 Organizing

OUTLINING

Making an outline can help you to organize your ideas before you write.

1 *Read the first part of an outline about Sorbian, a language spoken in Germany.*

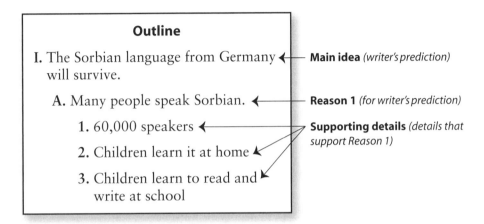

Outline

I. The Sorbian language from Germany will survive. — **Main idea** *(writer's prediction)*

   A. Many people speak Sorbian. — **Reason 1** *(for writer's prediction)*

      1. 60,000 speakers — **Supporting details** *(details that support Reason 1)*

      2. Children learn it at home

      3. Children learn to read and write at school

2 *Read the second part of the outline. Complete **B** (Reason 2) with a sentence from the box below. Choose the reason that is best supported by the details given.*

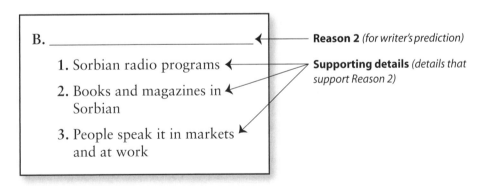

B. _____ — **Reason 2** *(for writer's prediction)*

   1. Sorbian radio programs — **Supporting details** *(details that support Reason 2)*

   2. Books and magazines in Sorbian

   3. People speak it in markets and at work

Sorbian is an old language.

Sorbian is useful in everyday life.

Most parents speak Sorbian to their children.

3 *Choose two languages from the Prewriting section (pages 72–74) that you want to write about: one language that you think will survive and one that won't. Use the information from the chart on page 74 to write an outline of your paragraphs. Include two reasons for your opinion about each language.*

Outline

I. The _____ language will survive.

    A. _____

        1. _____

        2. _____

    B. _____

        1. _____

        2. _____

II. The _____ language will not survive.

    A. _____

        1. _____

        2. _____

    B. _____

        1. _____

        2. _____

WRITING THE FIRST DRAFT

Use the information from the previous sections to write the first draft of your paragraphs.

- Write two paragraphs, one for each language.

- Begin each paragraph with a topic sentence that makes a prediction about whether or not the language will survive.

- Include at least two reasons for each prediction. Support the reasons with details from the FAQs on endangered languages in the Prewriting section.

Don't worry too much about grammar. Just try to make your ideas clear.

PEER REVIEW

When you finish your first draft, exchange papers with another student. Read your partner's first draft and answer the questions below. Then discuss your answers with your partner.

- Does the writer create two paragraphs, one for each language?

- Does the writer begin each paragraph with a topic sentence that predicts whether or not the language will survive?

- Does the writer include at least two reasons for each prediction?

- Do you agree with the writer's predictions? Why or why not?

Discuss your partner's reaction to your paragraphs. Make a note of any parts you need to revise.

---

3 Revising

A   WRITING A CONCLUDING SENTENCE

A concluding sentence can restate the main idea of the topic sentence. It can also suggest a solution or express an opinion.

1 *Read the paragraph. Then look at the three possible concluding sentences below. Write* ***R*** *(restates the main idea),* ***S*** *(makes a suggestion), or* ***O*** *(states an opinion) next to each.*

> I predict that Sorbian, a language spoken in Germany, will survive. There are several reasons for my opinion. First, many people speak Sorbian now. There are about 60,000 speakers. Also, most children learn Sorbian at home. They also learn to read and write Sorbian in some schools. These children will know the language, and they will teach it to their children. Another reason is that Sorbian is useful in everyday life. People can listen to Sorbian radio programs. They can read books and magazines in Sorbian. People speak Sorbian in the markets and at work. _____

_____ **1.** For these reasons, I believe that people will continue to speak the Sorbian language.

_____ **2.** In my opinion, the work to preserve the Sorbian language is very important.

_____ **3.** I think that the Sorbian people should continue their successful work to preserve the language.

2 *Look at the second draft of your paragraphs. Write concluding sentences for each paragraph.*

B EXPRESSING FUTURE PREDICTIONS WITH *WILL* AND *BE GOING TO*

Complete Unit 10, Section 4B, in the Student Book before you begin this section.

In your paragraphs, you can use *will* and *be going to* to make predictions about the future.

1 *Look at the following sentences. Fill in the correct future form of the verbs in parentheses to complete the prediction about each language.*

1. Some schools teach Sorbian. The children who attend these schools

   _____ bilingual.
   (be)

2. There are only 40 speakers of Hokkaido Ainu, a language in Japan. Most

   children _____ speaking the language.
   (not/grow up)

3. Linguists now make videotapes of fluent Potawatomi speakers. People

   _____ the videotapes and remember the language.
   (watch)

4. Wambaya, a language in Australia, only has 10 or 12 fluent speakers. They

   are all over the age of 60. I think Wambaya _____.
   (not/survive)

5. Linguists are trying to write down traditional stories from many cultures.

   This means people _____ the stories and can tell them to
   not/forget
   their children and grandchildren.

2 *Look at your first draft. Do you use **will** or **be going to** to write about the future? Underline all the places where you should use **will** or **be going to**.*

WRITING THE SECOND DRAFT

Now you are ready to write your second draft. Look at your notes from the previous sections to help you revise.

• Write a concluding sentence for each of the paragraphs.

• Use *will* and *be going to* to write about the future.

4 Editing

CORRECTING VERB FORMS

1 *Correct the verbs in each of the following sentences.*

       will or *are going to*
1. In the future, children be bilingual.

2. People going study the grammar.

3. Children know stories of the culture.

4. Adults are watch videotapes to help them remember.

5. Linguists are going study the language more.

2 *Look at your second draft. Are all the verb forms correct? Correct any verb form errors.*

PREPARING THE FINAL DRAFT

Carefully edit your second draft. Use the checklist below as a guide. Then neatly write or type your paragraphs with the corrections.

FINAL DRAFT CHECKLIST

❑ Do you have two paragraphs, one for each language?

❑ Does each paragraph have a topic sentence that makes a prediction about whether the language will survive?

❑ Do you have two reasons for your opinion about each language?

❑ Are there details from the FAQs on endangered languages to support each reason?

❑ Do you have a concluding sentence for each of the paragraphs?

❑ Do you use *will* and *be going to* to write about the future?

❑ Did you check the verb forms?

Answer Key

Note: For exercises where no answers are given, answers will vary.

UNIT 1

2 Organizing (page 3)

1 1. *Topic sentence:* I would like to be a mountain climbing guide.

   2. Mountain climbing is very exciting; I enjoy working outside; I like to meet interesting people.

2 *Topic sentence:* Sometimes I imagine I'm a veterinarian.

3 Revising (pages 4–5)
A

1 *Cross out:*

Sometimes children are difficult to work with because they don't always listen and follow directions.

Artists are creative too, so I would also like to be an artist.

But I don't like the salary, because teachers don't make very much money.

B

1 1. <u>Good</u> teachers are <u>creative</u>.
   2. They teach <u>interesting</u> classes.
   3. They are also <u>patient</u> and <u>caring</u>.

4 Editing (page 7)

1   My Ideal Job

Sometimes I imagine that I am a teacher. I like this job for several reasons. First, I love children. I like to help children learn and grow. Children are fun to work with because they like to laugh and play games. Second, teaching is a creative job. Teachers think of new and interesting ways to learn. Finally, the schedule is convenient for me. Teachers can take long vacations in the summer.

UNIT 2

2 Organizing (page 10)

1 Where you went: West Park

   What you did there: walked, jogged, rode my bike, looked around

What you saw: the lake, people riding bikes, buildings, people walking and jogging, ducks and geese, people fishing, people in-line skating, people boating, squirrels, boats

How you felt: happy, relaxed

3 Revising (pages 12–13)
A

1 a. Sometimes I rent a boat at the boathouse there.
      There are lots of ducks living on the lake.
      There are trails around the lake for walking and jogging.

   b. I always felt very relaxed there.
      The mountains were so quiet and life seemed so slow.
      The fresh air made me feel healthy.

   c. You can see many beautiful flowers and trees.
      The birds are always a pleasure to watch.
      It's fun to watch people walking, jogging, or riding their bicycles.

B

1 1. stayed   6. rode
   2. helped   7. saw
   3. fed   8. was
   4. watered   9. felt
   5. took

4 Editing (page 14)

1   Last Saturday, I went to a park in my neighborhood. It was a beautiful day. The park was very crowded. It was full of children, adults, and dogs. My friend and I rode our bikes to the park, played some Frisbee, and had a picnic lunch. Then we went home. It was a fun afternoon.

UNIT 3

1 Prewriting (page 16)

1 1. regular computer paper
   2. color-changing ink
   4. legal

2 Organizing (page 18)

1 1. There are several important differences between real money and counterfeit money.

2. The paper is different. The ink is different. The printing methods are also different.

3. In contrast (opposite idea), In addition (similar idea), However (opposite idea), also (similar idea), In contrast (opposite idea)

3 Revising (pages 20–21)

A

1 The special paper <u>has red and blue silk in it</u>. Color-changing ink <u>looks yellow from one angle and green from another</u>. Microprint <u>is the use of small words hidden in the design</u>.

B

1 1. rougher   2. easier

4 Editing (page 22)

1 *Corrected sentences with punctuation:*

<u>In addition</u>, it has a line that you can see with an ultraviolet light. <u>In contrast</u>, counterfeit money uses regular computer paper.

<u>However</u>, counterfeit money uses regular ink.

<u>In contrast</u>, counterfeit money doesn't have microprint.

UNIT 4

2 Organizing (page 25)

1 1. Yes. Yes.
2. No. No.
3. Yes. Yes.
4. No. Yes.
5. Yes. No.

Letters 1 and 3 will be the most persuasive because the writers explain who they are and why they are writing.

3 Opinion 1: Hunters kill tigers and sell their fur.
Tigers are an important part of our ecology.
Today, there are only between 5,000 and 7,000 wild tigers in the world.

Opinion 2: Tigers hunt and kill people.
People cannot have farms where tigers live.

3 Revising (pages 27–28)

A

1 1. The first example is vague without exact numbers. It also states an opinion. The second example is not about tigers. The third example gives specific numbers. It is the most persuasive.

2. The first example doesn't explain why dolphins are intelligent. The second example explains dolphins' intelligence and why we should save them. It is the most persuasive. The third example is not about dolphins.

B

1 Why should we save them?
How are they important?
What can you do?

2 We must act now to save the endangered wild tigers. <u>Why should we save them</u>? First, tigers are beautiful animals. They are the biggest cats in the world. They are known everywhere for their beautiful orange and black striped fur. In addition, tigers are an important part of our ecology. <u>How are they important</u>? They hunt and kill small animals such as rats and rabbits. Without tigers, the number of small animals would increase and cause problems for people. Finally, we don't have much time to save the tigers. <u>How many tigers are there</u>? There are only between 5,000 and 7,000 wild tigers in the world today. One hundred years ago there were over 100,000 tigers. Some experts say that in ten years, wild tigers will be extinct. <u>What can you do</u>? Join the fight to save the endangered wild tigers!

4 Editing (page 29)

2 **Openings:** Dear Editor: / To Whom It May Concern:
Closings: Sincerely, / Yours Truly,

UNIT 5

1 Prewriting (page 31)

2 *Add the information to the tree diagram in this order:*
Write to several people at the same time.
Fast answers to messages.
Cheaper than a phone call.
Can't hear a person's tone of voice.
Send private information by mistake.
Computer modem to connect to the Internet.

2 Organizing (pages 32–33)

1 1. You can work when everyone is sleeping. You can work when you have time.

2. You need a computer. You need to have an Internet service provider.

2 *Add the sentences in this order:*

I often get an immediate reply.

I know people who live in many parts of the world, and I can send e-mail to all of them.

You can choose the wrong e-mail address if you are not careful and send the e-mail to the wrong person.

You can't hear a person's tone of voice.

3 Revising (pages 34–35)

A

1 *Cross out:* b, d

2 1. *Topic sentence:* Two-way text pagers have advantages and disadvantages.

2. *Two advantages:* They are convenient. They are quiet.

Two disadvantages: The keys are very small. The print is small.

3. *Cross out:* However, my mother doesn't have one, so I have to call her on the telephone.

My friend has a pager that makes a lot of funny noises.

I wish I took typing in college.
It's easier to read messages on the computer.

4 Editing (page 37)

2 1. E-mail has several disadvantages: it takes too much time, it is not personal, and there are too many misunderstandings.

2. My sister, mother, and brother all use cell phones.

3. Pagers are fast, easy, and fun to use.

4. I like to stay up late, listen to music, and answer all my e-mail.

5. There are some disadvantages to e-mail: I can't take type, I don't have an e-mail address, and I don't have a computer.

6. My family lives more than 3,000 miles away. I can still stay in touch by e-mail.

UNIT 6

1 Prewriting (page 40)

1 1. c 2. b

2 Organizing (pages 41–42)

1 1. *Topic sentence:* I agree with this proverb because married couples often have different opinions about housework.

2. *General statement:* Couples often have different opinions about housework.

3. The writer uses her personal experience as an example.

2 1. S 2. G 3. G 4. S 5. S 6. G

3 General statement _2_ is supported by example _1_ .
General statement _3_ is supported by example _5_ .
General statement _6_ is supported by example _4_ .

3 Revising (page 43)

A

1 *Concluding sentence:* Housework can make marriage difficult.

2 1. d 2. a 3. b 4. c

4 Editing (page 45)

1 1. <u>And around the house</u>. Many men work full time and help around the house.

2. <u>Cook, clean, and go to my job everyday</u>. I work harder than my husband. I cook, clean, and go to my job every day.

3. <u>Work together to cook and clean</u>. My mother and father share the housework. They work together to cook and clean.

4. <u>And earn more money</u>. Men work harder than women and earn more money.

UNIT 7

2 Organizing (pages 49–50)

1 1. S 2. C 3. B 4. C 5. S 6. S 7. C 8. C

2 1. C 2. S 3. S 4. C 5. C 6. S

3 Revising (pages 52–53)

A

1 1. e 2. f 3. g 4. h 5. d 6. b 7. c 8. a

3 1. c 2. g 3. e 4. b 5. f 6. d 7. h 8. a

B

1 1. The Stinking Rose is *a* famous restaurant in Beverly Hills.

2. *Bagna calda* is made from garlic cloves roasted in olive oils and butter.

3. It is served with breads.

4. The desserts don't have *any* ~~some~~ garlic in them.

5. They serve *a* lot of delicious food.

6. They sell ~~a~~ tools for preparing and cooking garlic.

7. The chef has worked at ~~any~~ *some* famous restaurants.

8. The Stinking Rose is ^*an*^ interesting restaurant.

4 Editing (page 54)

1 1. Some of their famous dishes include *bagna calda,* which is garlic cloves roasted in olive oil and butter. It's served with bread.

2. I tried the neon ravioli, which is filled with cheese and garlic. There are also seafood dishes including a delicious baked salmon with garlic.

3. Prices are reasonable. Appetizers are from $6.00 to $9.50. Entrees are from $10.50 to $15.00.

4. Service is excellent. It is very fast.

UNIT 8

2 Organizing (pages 58–59)

1 Outline: I. A. 1. b. Flight is nonstop

A. 2. b. Can get to airports by driving, going on subway, or taking shuttle bus

B. 1. a. Planes often late

II. A. 1. a. Trip takes more than eight hours

A. 2. a. Seats are small and hard

B. 1. a. Can stop and visit towns along the way.

3 Revising (pages 61–62)

A

1 *Combine with the following connectors:*

1. and 2. but 3. and 4. but 5. but 6. and

B

1 1. b. You can relax on the train.

c. You can't be in a hurry.

2. a. You can make your own schedule.

b. You can stop when you want.

c. You can't sleep while you travel.

3. a. You can help reduce pollution.

b. You can get some exercise.

c. You can stop and look at things along the way.

4 Editing (page 63)

1 1. You can relax on the train, and you don't have to look at a map for directions.

2. The train is slower than flying, but you can see the beautiful scenery along the way.

3. The bus is cheap, but it makes a lot of stops. In addition, it is often crowded, and it can be very uncomfortable.

4. Flying is the fastest, but it can cost the most. You can find cheap tickets, but tickets are more expensive during popular travel times.

5. Riding a bicycle is a good way to help reduce air pollution, and you can get some exercise.

UNIT 9

1 Prewriting (page 66)

2 The man's problem: He's overweight.

Product name: Thin-Fast Diet Tea

What the product does: It helps you to lose weight, even when you eat a lot.

What it's made of: All-natural tea and herbs

What it's like (description): It tastes sweet and delicious; it smells like oranges and lemons.

How you use it: Put it in boiling water. Drink it two times a day until you lose all the weight you want.

Comment from a happy customer: "It's terrific! It really works! I lost weight and now I feel great!"

2 Organizing (page 67)

1 1, 4, 2, 3

3 Revising (pages 69–70)

A

1 1. It tastes like chocolate.

2. It is fast and easy to use.

3. It smells like spring flowers.

4. It looks like a tiny pill.

5. It is convenient.

6. It tastes terrific.

B

1 1. You should drink Thin-Fast twice a day, once in the morning and once in the evening.

2. You should continue to drink Thin-Fast every day until you lose all the weight you want.

3. You shouldn't spend another day dieting and exercising.

4. You should buy some today!

4 Editing (page 71)

1
1. One customer said, "Thin-Fast changed my life!"
2. "I feel happy and full of energy," Mary Ann said.
3. Customers who use Thin-Fast say, "It's terrific! It really works!"
4. I asked, "What do you think of Thin-Fast?"

UNIT 10

2 Organizing (page 78)

B

2 Sorbian is useful in everyday life.

3 Revising (pages 77–78)

A

1 1. R   2. O   3. S

B

1 1. will be;   2. will not/won't grow up;   3. will watch;   4. will not/won't survive;   5. will not/won't forget

4 Editing (page 79)

1
2. People *are* going to study the grammar.
3. Children *will* know stories of the culture.
4. Adults are *going to* watch videotapes to help them remember.
5. Linguists are going *to* study the language more.

Notes

Notes

Notes

Notes